Let's
wildflower
the world

Let's wildflower the world

Save, swap and seedbomb to rewild our world

Josie Jeffery

Quotes

"Anticipation and pleasure encapsulate the essence of seed swapping for me. Sowing new acquisitions obtained from fellow enthusiasts who had a glint in their eye of the beauty or the food that they were sharing. Hopefully, the next generation of pleasure-seeking seed swappers is well on its way and this lovely book will keep them on the path of discovery."

Andy Jackson

FORMER HEAD OF WAKEHURST,
ROYAL BOTANIC GARDENS, KEW

"The Soil Association recognises the importance of conserving, not only the genetic diversity of our food supply, but also the skills and knowledge of saving seed in growers both professional and amateur. We have already lost thousands of varieties due to the concentration of seed production in a relatively small number of companies and this trend is set to continue. Home saving and swapping of seed is one way to fight against this and retain some sovereignty and ownership of what we grow and eat."

Ben Raskin

HEAD OF HORTICULTURE, SOIL
ASSOCIATION

"Seeds are the source of life and this book will help you to reach that source."

Satish Kumar

EDITOR-IN-CHIEF,
RESURGENCE & THE ECOLOGIST

"There is little doubt that this book will be a 'must have' reference at Seedy Sunday. It will fit into a large pocket or bag. It is not only a delight to hold and beautiful to browse through, but a source of valuable information for use on a coffee table, as a reference source at any Seedy Sunday or for me to keep in my allotment shed."

Alan Phillips

CHAIRPERSON, SEEDY SUNDAY, BRIGHTON

"There is nothing more important in our times than saving seeds and swapping seeds. We are faced with a seed emergency caused by rapid disappearance of seed diversity, the replacement of renewable seeds with non-renewable, patented seeds, and the perverse idea that seed saving and seed sharing is an 'intellectual property crime'. Seedswap will help spread the seeds of freedom."

Dr Vandana Shiva

SEED ACTIVIST & FOUNDER OF
NAVDANYA INTERNATIONAL

"The amount of interest in seed swaps is growing all the time and it's great to see a book that not only tells you about the 'why do' but also the 'how to' of seed swapping and the practical art of saving seeds as well."

Neil Munro

MANAGER, THE HERITAGE SEED LIBRARY

Contents

Foreword

It's easy to forget the extraordinary wonders of nature. The story of Jack and the Beanstalk is an entertaining fairy tale that one generation of parents after another read to their children. The cycle of nature is repeated and renewed with relish, as the beanstalk never fails to inspire awe in little children. How can such a small bean grow so tall that it reaches out to the heavens?

As a gardener and seed saver, I take it for granted that a small tomato seed, less than three millimetres in diameter, can grow within months to a plant a metre high and wide, with scores of deliciously warm, sun-blessed tomatoes, such as Gardeners' Delight or Brandywine, that are just asking to be eaten.

Many adults, even gardeners, consider seed sowing, let alone seed saving and storing, to be black arts and they stand in awe of those who have these skills. Now Seedswap shares all, bursting the bubble of those myths, and showing how all careful gardeners can and should save and sow their own seeds. Seed saving, storing and sowing all require some care and nurturing to ensure that plants remain true and strong. One of the great strengths of this book is that it covers all three aspects, while almost half of it showcases a wide variety of plants from which seed can be saved.

Seed saving and sowing are a crucial part of a much wider sustainability and self-reliance agenda, where 'small is beautiful' and where we must think globally and act locally. Ever since mankind evolved from being hunter-gatherers to farmers, communities have had a vested interest in ensuring the quality and security of food supplies. This included the saving, storing and sowing of the most reliable and productive varieties of crops.

Multinational companies that often export and import food across continents have also recognised the importance of seed varieties that not only produce crops that can be transported easily, but also have a long shelf-life in shops and look good any time of the year. These companies often create a monopoly on certain seeds (F1 hybrid varieties, for example), which have to be bought from them; it becomes uneconomic for them to sell a wide variety of seeds, especially ones that have adapted over generations to a local environment.

Seed saving and swapping can be great fun too. The Seedy Sunday event in Brighton started just over a decade ago on the first Sunday in February. Now thousands of people come out of their winter hibernation for this community event, to swap seeds, meet old friends, buy seed potatoes, obtain heritage varieties, have coffee and cake and listen to talks. See www.seedysunday.org.

There is little doubt that this book will be a 'must have' reference at Seedy Sunday. It is not only a delight to hold and beautiful to browse through, but a source of valuable information for use on a coffee table, a reference source at any Seedy Sunday or for me to keep in my allotment shed.

Alan Phillips
CHAIRPERSON, SEEDY SUNDAY, BRIGHTON

Kew Introduction

Seeds give plants a world-crossing mobility: a resilient, agile package encoded to start growing only in optimum conditions. Seeds are the plant world's agents of change, an adaptable, versatile biological phenomenon.

Seeds allow plants to diversify, a method of reproduction capable of generating subtle differences from the parent plant. These differences can hold the secret to future fitness: generating traits such as drought tolerance and disease resistance. A large seed-raised population of a single species may have multiple adaptations to a climatic or biological threat, increasing chances of survival.

Humanity has harnessed the potential of seeds for tens of thousands of years. Evidence from California shows that pre-agrarian societies were harvesting, selecting and distributing seeds of wild plants, influencing how and where species grew. As we began to cultivate plants more intensively, our instincts to select, collect, cultivate, harvest and eat tied our livelihoods inexorably to seeds. Most of our global calories now derive from seeds: wheat, rice and maize, and it's the energy

reserves and ease of storage of the plant world's agents of change we now value the most.

Seeds not only feed the world, they also provide an empowering, democratic resource for gardeners too. A handful of seeds can transform bare earth into a beautiful sea of colour or produce a tasty crop for a few pence. Seeds put landscape change in the hands of the many, powering food-growing initiatives, city greening and community wildflower meadows. Seeds have an intrinsic value, a package of potential with the power to delight – an ageless, classless gift. Seeds swapping connects us to our ancestry, where seeds were the most desirable of currencies.

However, we have an inherent duty to be responsible in our choice of species. Seeds can transform for good and ill and care must be exercised in what we choose to sow and where. Our global ecosystems have taken a heavy toll from thoughtless plant introductions and selfish sowings as our desired species, free from ecological constraint, have morphed into invasive rogues. Japanese knotweed, Himalayan balsam, Lantana and Eucalyptus are stark living reminders of the dangers of poorly chosen introductions. The Global Species Invasiveness Database (http://www. iucngisd.org/gisd/)is an invaluable guide to what not to sow and is free to use.

The American Prairie at Kew's wild botanic garden at Wakehurst is a seed-powered large-scale landscape of wonder. Translating three wild US plant communities into a 6-acre designed landscape, we used ecologically informed methods to make it establish robustly and be stable for decades to come. All our American Prairie species were carefully screened for potential invasiveness, a painstaking 6-month process. Once selected and sourced, we sowed a base layer of grasses and pioneering prairie plants direct into the ground. A resilient swathe of approximately 15 million seedlings emerged, a true survival of the fittest. Fully adapted to their conditions, these seedlings withstood frost, drought and downpours, only growing when the conditions allowed. A regular regime of bison-replicating mows encouraged the young crop to root and give room to new emergents.

A total of 50,000 nursery-raised plants were then added into the tightly cropped swathe. Collected in the wilds of Illinois as seeds, these were the plants that required a helping hand to establish, with nourishing compost and a protective glasshouse environment guaranteeing good establishment. As the direct-sown and nursery-raised plants grow together, under gentle disturbance from us, they'll find complementary niches and become a community.

Seeds allow all of us to become gardeners. With little space or money we can experience that first, visceral experience of growth and new life, an empowering sense that food or beauty is in our hands to make.

Ed Ikin FRSA

DIRECTOR OF WAKEHURST,
ROYAL BOTANIC GARDENS, KEW

Author Introduction

You might ask the question: why do we need to wildflower the world? The simple answer is that if we don't, the world will no longer be able to survive. Every living thing on this planet has a symbiotic relationship with another living organism, which is how harmony is maintained. This harmony has been off-balance for many years and industrialisation has wiped out many wildlife habitats. We can all do our bit and join together to actively create micro-habitats using native wildflower seeds in our gardens, in our streets, in our schools and outside our offices. This will help to create food sources for our wildlife, which will have an immediate effect: bees will return to our skies and dance from flower to flower, indicating to other flying insects that there is nectar in these parts; small mammals will scurry towards the action to eat the insects and seeds; in turn, they will create a nutrient-rich compost for when the seeds are ready to fall to the ground, and more plants will grow. It has been scientifically proven that a tomato tastes better when it has been pollinated by a native bee, so it's a win-win situation.

Contributing to wildlife habitats in your everyday routine is easy and can be done in small or big steps. I hope that you find this book useful to help you along on your eco-warrior journey.

Josie and her Roots

I had a creative, musical and unusual upbringing. My family home was made from wood and metal and had wheels! I lived in a bus with my family and was home educated. I'm the second of five children – the others are Amy, Arran, Holly and Rose.

During the late 1970s and 80s, we travelled around Europe in a convoy or on our own and busked as a family band to make a living. We went to festivals such as Stonehenge and Glastonbury, squatted on land and travelled with circuses.

We used to rest from our travels at a commune in Suffolk called Brick Kiln Farm, where we grew our own food and reared chickens and pigs. Brick Kiln Farm ran a charity called Green Deserts and grew trees in nurseries on the farm.

I remember running around barefoot at the Rougham Tree Fair, their charity fundraiser, and getting up to all sorts of mischief! Green Deserts' inspiring ethos was to re-fertilise desert wastelands using natural energy technology and organic plant husbandry.

My family settled in Wales in 1990 at a friend's farm, and in 1991 we bought some Welsh land – somewhere to anchor our roots. Arran, Holly and Rose went to school, while Amy and I began college. I studied art and met Steve, the father of my three sons, Tyrone, Isaac and George.

In 2003 we moved to Brighton, where – inspired by my love of watching things grow – I studied horticulture, then garden design. I began designing gardens that were slightly unruly and anarchistic. I veered towards recycled materials, wayward plants and graffiti murals.

During college I had a job at a local plant nursery and also helped run children's gardening workshops at the Museum of Garden History in London. I heard the word 'seedbomb' on the radio and a 'ping' moment happened – next thing I knew, we were doing seedbomb workshops in the museum. I set up my business seedfreedom in 2008 and spent 10+ years teaching people about habitat restoration, seedbomb making and seed saving at workshops, festivals, fairs, art projects, schools, organisations and charities.

I have always been fascinated by the relationship between wildlife and food growing, for example, the fact that native insects pollinating tomatoes make the fruit sweeter (see my book *Good Companions*). I am passionate about food waste and food poverty issues. Over the years I have met many wonderful micro-producers and in 2014 I set up a workers' co-op called 'Foodshed' in Brighton Open Market selling zero-waste food and renting shelves to micro-producers. I was in the market for 5 years before I went on to work as a volunteer manager, first with the YMCA and then during the Covid-19 pandemic, for FareShare Sussex, a charity that tackles food waste and food poverty issues by redistributing surplus food to the needy.

Gardening is a huge part of my life and being in nature is how I replenish my energy levels and connect to my environment. In this strange and challenging world, it is important to spend time outdoors, to gain perspective and find peace, and for me that can be found by walking through meadows and watching bees dancing from flower to flower or noticing seedlings springing up from a mossy woodland floor.

Find me on Instagram @and_sow_we_grow

Chapter 1

AN INTRODUCTION TO SEEDS

Seeds: Their Purpose & Importance

Seeds are the source of life. They support our ecosystems and enable flowering plants to avoid extinction. They're also a source of food for humans and animals, in seed and in fruit and vegetable form.

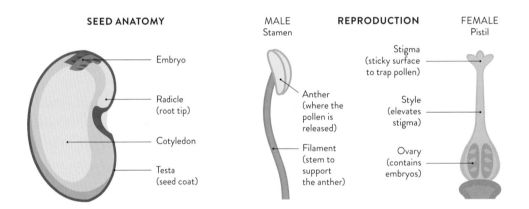

SEED ANATOMY

- Embryo
- Radicle (root tip)
- Cotyledon
- Testa (seed coat)

MALE
Stamen

- Anther (where the pollen is released)
- Filament (stem to support the anther)

REPRODUCTION

FEMALE
Pistil

- Stigma (sticky surface to trap pollen)
- Style (elevates stigma)
- Ovary (contains embryos)

Seeds

A seed contains an embryo (unborn plant), which is formed in the ovary of a flower. The embryo is surrounded by the testa, a protective coat, which nourishes and prevents the seed from drying out, and protects it from any mechanical injuries that might occur after dispersal.

The sole purpose of a plant is to reproduce. There are male and female reproductive parts of the flower. Most flowers have both, but some flowers are single sex, such as pumpkin flowers. Some plants can reproduce vegetatively, by producing offsets and runners, but in most cases, seed production is the most effective way of ensuring the genetic diversity and long-term success of a species. Seeds are a food source to wildlife (and humans) and many of them won't reach germination. So, as an insurance, an individual plant can produce tens, hundreds and even thousands of seeds.

For a flowering plant to produce seeds it has to work in partnership with nature and adapt in ways that will attract

ABOVE The basic parts of a typical seed.

RIGHT This pink campion uses its bright petals to attract insect pollinators. The seed head swells until it reaches maturity. It will dry in the sun and turn brown. The crown peels back to reveal tiny black seeds which will be wind dispersed into the garden.

partners such as insects, bees, butterflies, small mammals and birds.

Insects help by transferring pollen from the anther to the stigma, thus enabling fertilization so that seeds can form in the ovary. The most effective way for plants to attract pollinators is to produce colourful flowers with dazzling patterns and seductive scents. The pollinators are rewarded with sweet nectar. Plants that are grown out of their natural habitat, away from their native pollinators, usually have introduced pollinators or are pollinated artificially by hand.

The shape, location and size of seeds varies greatly between species and depends on the dispersal method. For example, some wind-carried seeds are winged or feathered; others are formed within or on the outside of brightly coloured fruit to entice birds and small mammals. Whether they pass through an animal or travel across the skies and the seas, the seed's sole purpose is to spread itself as widely as possible. For millennia, humans have played their own important role in seed dispersal by collecting, growing and storing seeds – a tradition that continues today with seed swapping.

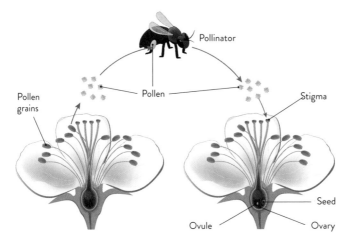

POLLINATION

Pollinator

Pollen grains

Pollen

Stigma

Ovule

Seed

Ovary

Pollination & Fertilization

Pollination is a significant part of the reproduction process of flowering plants, where pollen is transferred from an anther to a stigma. It enables fertilization and the consequent formation of seeds. Some flowers are able to pollinate themselves (self-pollination), whereas others will only accept pollen from a separate plant.

› The stigma traps a grain of pollen, which germinates into a pollen tube and grows down the style and into the ovary.
› The pollen tube reaches an ovule and releases two male cells.
› One cell combines with the ovule, the second combines with the polar nuclei and later becomes the endosperm (food supply).
› Fertilization occurs.
› Once the ovule, or ovules, have been fertilized, the flower is no longer needed and the petals and stamens will wither.
› Seed maturity can take roughly 25–30 days.
› The fertilized egg develops into an embryo contained within the seed.
› Ovules at the time of fertilization are white and eventually turn pale green as the seed enlarges during its early stages of development.

› Each seed is attached to the ovary wall by a stalk, from which it receives the food to fuel its growth.
› As the seeds develop, the ovary enlarges becoming recognisable as a fruit or seed pod.

The development of the fruit differs from plant to plant; some seeds develop within a wet fruit, such as an aubergine or tomato, and some develop within a dry seed pod, such as a poppy seed head or pea pod.

ABOVE Diagram explaining the process of insect pollination.

RIGHT Open sunflower head.

BELOW Some seeds, such as pumpkin seeds, are wet and others, such as peas, are dry seeds.

Hand-Pollination

In hand-pollination, people intervene to control the pollination process. This may simply be because there are no pollinators present (if, for example, plants are grown in a glasshouse), but usually the purpose is to enable the parent plants to produce 'true' seeds. Gardeners can transfer pollen with a brush, or use a cotton bud to swab the pollen from the anthers onto the stigma. Self-pollinating plants can be shaken, which loosens the pollen allowing it to be transferred in the air, or flowers can be simply rubbed together. There are varying methods that have been developed for specific plants. Two methods are described here:

Curcubit Technique

Curcubits, such as cucumber and pumpkin, have separate male and female flowers on the same plant. The female flower has an ovary that resembles an undeveloped fruit at its base. The male flower lacks this feature, simply having a thin stalk. To keep your seeds 'true', follow these steps:

1 Before dusk, locate male and female flowers from the same plant.
2 To prevent insects from flying in, use masking tape to shut the tips of the flowers that are about to open the next morning.
3 When the morning dew has dried the following day, pluck off the male flower leaving a short stem. Gently remove the tape and all the petals, leaving only the anthers, turning the male flower into a pollen paintbrush!

4 Carefully remove the tape from the female flower and allow it to open. Swipe the pollen brush onto the female stigma.
5 Re-tape the female flower and securely mark the stem with colourful waterproof string.
6 The eventual fruit will be the one from which you save your 'true' seed.

Sunflower Technique

1 Cover two flower heads each with a porous bag before the florets open to prevent them from being accessed by pollinating insects.
2 Seal them around the flower stalks with tape. When the flowers start shedding pollen, remove one of the bags and gently rub the flower head with a soft bristled brush.
3 Remove the bag from the other flower head, and use the same brush to brush another flower.
4 Re-bag the flower heads swiftly after pollinating to exclude the chance of any further pollination by insects or birds.
5 The florets open in succession, so brush the same flower heads daily for up to two weeks.

Germination

Germination is a process by which the embryo of a plant grows on from the seed stage to the seedling stage. Three factors must be fulfilled before a seed will germinate:

1 **SEED VIABILITY** The embryo must first be alive.
2 **SEED DORMANCY** Dormancy must be overcome; some seeds will remain dormant until they have experienced certain conditions, such as being passed through the digestive system of an animal or going through a period of cold, soaking, scarification or fermentation.
3 **ENVIRONMENTAL CONDITIONS** These include oxygen, temperature, light and water levels.

The Phases

As a seed germinates, it goes through three phases before it sprouts into a seedling.

1 **WATER IMBIBITION** Water triggers germination. The embryo within the seed absorbs water and causes it to swell until the testa bursts.
2 **THE LAG PHASE** The cells prepare for growth, adjusting to the environment but not actively dividing.
3 **RADICLE EMERGENCE** The stage in which the seedling root (radicle) emerges from the seed.

Radicle emergence is considered the completion of germination and the plant then moves towards the seedling stage.

Viability

In seed terms, the definition of viability is 'the potential to germinate'. The length a seed stays viable for varies from plant to plant, but correct storage conditions can increase its chances of successful future germination.

The oldest recorded seed to be germinated was from a Judean date palm, resurrected in 2005 from a 2,000-year-old seed at the Louis L. Borick Natural Medicine Research Center, Israel.

Some seeds have an extended longevity, enabling them to exist in the 'soil seed bank' for many years before the right conditions present themselves for germination.

Dormancy

A seed remains dormant (inactive) to ensure minimal risk of failure. It is a way of enduring until conditions are optimal for germination and the survival of the seedling. Dormancy will only break if the conditions are just right: when the soil is moist enough and the temperature is correct. For example, some plants from arid parts of the world and some grasses need a period of low moisture and will only germinate after a period of drying.

Not all seeds, even if they are of the same variety, break their dormancy at exactly the same time. This is a fairly common adaptation, which enables plants to avoid any potential threats like late frosts or being eaten. It is nature's way of making sure some seedlings survive.

Dormancy Types

MORPHOLOGICAL Here, the embryo is underdeveloped at dispersal. Germination will be prevented until the embryo is fully developed.

PHYSIOLOGICAL Chemical inhibitors prevent the embryo from breaking through the seed coat. Dormancy will only break when external environmental factors, such as sunlight or high temperatures, cause these inhibitors to break down.

MORPHOPHYSIOLOGICAL These seeds have underdeveloped embryos and physiological restraints. They may need dormancy-breaking treatments such as stratification, scarification or soaking.

PHYSICAL This is when the seed coats are hard, making them impermeable to water. The seed may need to undergo some kind of physical or chemical process before dormancy is broken, such as passing through an animal's digestive system.

TOP You can see the emerging radicle on these lentil seeds.

BOTTOM As soon as the seed leaves rise, they begin to photosynthesise, which helps fuel the growth of these little seedlings.

Heritage vs Hybrid Seeds

Plants will adapt their seeds in order to survive in a world that is ever-changing and evolving. In nature, this can happen slowly as the climate changes and new threats, such as disease, are introduced. But humans have developed ways to speed up these natural adaptations.

Heritage

This is a term used for plants grown over multiple generations whose seeds are kept 'true' by conventional breeding. They are often difficult to find in the commercial seed trade because they are not deemed commercially viable. Some heritage varieties have been passed on for hundreds of years, and they usually succeed if they possess a superior virtue, such as flavour, colour or texture. They may lack resistance to certain pests and diseases, but the genetic variety they offer make them an important resource that plant breeders may need to draw on in the future. All heritage seeds must be open-pollinated.

What is Open-pollinated?

These are varieties that will grow 'true' from seed and are pollinated openly by wind and insects. They naturally cross breed with other closely related plants and the resulting seeds will not be 'true'. Open-pollinated plants are often well adapted to their local climate and can create their own 'natural' hybrids. Open-pollinated plants are the best for saving seeds, and in most cases, their seeds are the only ones accepted in seed swaps.

Advantages

› Free seeds are produced from year to year and from generation to generation.

› More stable traits are transferred from one plant generation to the next.
› Preservation of heritage plant varieties and a larger gene pool for future breeding.
› The crop is likely to mature over a longer period, making gluts less likely.
› In many cases, flavour and texture are improved.

Disadvantages

› Varieties will self- and cross-pollinate, which can lead to a loss of certain traits. You will need to intervene to prevent this in order to produce 'true' seed.
› 'Genetic drift' can happen over time and may make plant varieties 'deviate' too far from their accepted standard. Removal of these rogue plants will stop them from pollinating other plants and producing too much variation.

Hybrid

Charles Darwin began the hybrid revolution by suggesting that plants mutate and adapt over time in order to survive, and that any environmentally superior traits are passed on to their offspring. This is called natural selection. Prior to Darwin, however, farmers had been artificially selecting the seeds of their best plants, and over time this resulted in domesticated crops. Hybridisation will

happen in the wild, and it is often seen when two previously isolated plants are brought together, either by natural or by artificial means.

Today, plant breeders hybridise plants all the time in an effort to create a perfect plant with desirable traits. Such a hybrid is given an 'F1' status, which means it is the first filial generation of two specific male and female parent varieties. F1 seeds are 'super seeds' with specific desirable characteristics from both parents. Many common vegetables like aubergines, tomatoes, melons and bell peppers are F1 hybrids. These varieties are often selected for their productivity and ability to withstand the long-haul trips to supermarkets. Flavour and variety are often secondary concerns.

Advantages
› Wider adaptability to environmental stress.
› Greater uniformity among plants, and higher yields from food crops.
› Improved resistance to pests and diseases.
› Higher survival at the seedling stage.

Disadvantages
› Seeds cannot be saved from year to year as they will not be true to type.
› Their popularity is contributing to the extinction of heritage varieties.
› Lack of genetic variety.
› In many cases, the taste of F1 hybrid vegetables and fruit can be bland compared to heritage varieties.
› Breeding is costly and time consuming; therefore the seeds are more expensive.
› Patent laws can mean that if the wind accidentally blows patented F1 hybrid seeds on to your land and they grow there, there is a chance you are breaking the law.
› Uniformity of cropping means that gluts are more likely at harvest time.

ABOVE Corn, so essential to the world's food supply, was the first crop to be hybridised in the USA in the 1930s.

Genetically Modified Seeds

A genetically modified (GM) seed is the offspring of a plant whose genetic characteristics have been altered by the insertion of a modified gene or a gene from another organism through genetic engineering. It is a modern form of plant breeding that bypasses the more traditional methods.

'Seeds of Discontent'

Though the methods of GM are different, the aims are the same: to enhance existing desirable traits and to introduce new ones.

Some scientists believe that GM crops will help combat worldwide famine by producing plants with higher tolerances resulting in fewer risks of failure. Genetic engineering is potentially fast and very accurate; for example, by identifying the gene responsible for drought tolerance and modifying it, in theory, the desired traits will then be passed on to the offspring.

Genes from non-plant organisms can also be transferred. One famous example is the use of modified genes from a naturally occurring soil bacteria, *Bacillus thuringiensis* (Bt), in corn. These genes caused the corn plants to produce crystallised proteins that are lethal to a certain caterpillar pest that feeds on the crops. Plants that contain the *B. thuringiensis* gene are considered safe for human consumption, and safe for the environment, although this is a new science and research and debate is still continuing.

Many people have a strong opinion about GM foods, from environmental activists and religious organisations to scientists, government officials and the companies that create them. In theory, the science behind GM crops could do a lot of good for the world, by improving food supply and reducing the use of agrochemicals, but the environmental hazards and the risk to human health posed by GM technology, as well as the vested economic and political interests, are all high concerns.

Risks

› Chemicals expressed by GM genes could have an unexpected effect on other organisms, including humans. For example in the USA, pollen from Bt corn is believed to cause high mortality rates in Monarch butterfly caterpillars, which were not the target pest.

› GM plants may create new allergens. For example, a proposal to incorporate a gene from Brazil nuts into soya beans was abandoned in case it caused an allergic reaction when consumed.

› GM crops may cross-pollinate with natural crops and wild relatives, which could lead to widespread genetic contamination. If such genes were engineered for herbicide tolerance, crossing with related weed species might result in herbicide-tolerant 'superweeds'. Producing GM foods is lengthy and costly, which could result in consumers paying higher prices for food.

RIGHT Petri dish with germinated bean seedling growing in soil.

Seed Dispersal

There are many resourceful ways a plant can form to aid the dispersal of the seed in the most efficient way. The plant adapts into shapes and sizes that achieve the maximum chances of dispersal and this is dependent on where the plant likes to grow.

Below are a few ways that a seed can travel some distance from the parent plant to its new growing place.

Wind

Some seeds develop a shape that will enable them to be carried by the wind, such as dandelion parachutes, which have feathery hairs that help them travel long distances.

Maple keys, which have developed propeller-like wings, spin as they fall from the tree and can be taken off by the wind.

And some flowers, such as red campion, transform into a pepper-pot form that releases the seeds from small holes when the wind blows the stem.

Water

Plants that grow by the water rely on water to carry seeds to new locations, such as the palm with its floating coconut fruits or sea kale (*Crambe maritima*). They can travel long distances this way and will either germinate in the water or when they eventually become lodged in a muddy bank.

Explosive

As they dry, some plant pods will open explosively and expel their seeds – plants from the *Leguminosae* family, for example, like gorse and pea. As the pods are drying, a tension forms in the wall of the pod, which eventually releases like a tight spring and flicks away the seeds.

Hitch-hiking

Some seeds have developed sticky hooks or spines, which attach to passing animals or humans and hitch a ride for great distances – for example, burdock and goose grass!

Edible

Yummy fruits are the perfect way to entice animals – they eat the fruit and hidden inside are the seeds. Those seeds which cannot be digested are then expelled as droppings.

Some seeds cannot germinate unless they have been through the digestive system of an animal, as there are acids present that help break down the hard testa.

TOP The light and feathery hairs of the dandelion seed allow them to take flight when the wind blows.

BOTTOM RIGHT Small holes at the top of the poppy head allow seeds to be dispersed when disturbed by wind or person.

BOTTOM LEFT It is through being eaten that some fruits disperse their seeds.

Harvesting Seeds

The best way of building up your seed collection is to harvest them directly from plants. When you collect from the wild you are going straight to the source – it tells you the conditions that plant will thrive in, how big it grows, when it flowers, and when it sets seed.

The Best Time

Harvest seeds when the flower has died and the pod is ripe and swollen. Sometimes the petals are absent or have died and turned brown or black. It varies from plant to plant and happens throughout the summer and into the autumn months.

If you collect the seeds just before they would disperse naturally, you know they will be ripe. Read the plant profiles to find out when the plant sets seed.

The Right Way

This varies and is dependent on the type of fruit. With red campion, for example, the seeds are wind-dispersed and the openings appear as the seed pod dries; you can therefore collect the seed just before the openings appear in the pod. This will enable you to collect larger numbers of seed.

If you are a keen collector, take the following whenever you go for a country walk:

› PAPER BAGS
› STRING
› SECATEURS OR SCISSORS
› PENCIL OR PEN
› CAMERA

Harvesting Technique

The harvesting technique is simple and applies to most of the plants in this book.

1 **PHOTOGRAPH** the plant you harvest from.
2 **LABEL** each bag even if you don't know what the plant is. Note down distinctive features to help identify your crop when you get home – for example 'blue thistle-like flowers but no spikes on leaves'.
3 **CUT** the seed pod/head off, leaving at least 20cm of stem if possible.
4 **PLACE** in the labelled paper bag with the pods facing down. When you have a good bunch of about 20 stems, tie the bag around the stems.
5 **STORE** the bags suspended anywhere that is dry and warm. I dry them in my kitchen and airing cupboard.
6 **TIME** taken for the pods to be dry enough to release the seeds into the bag also varies from plant to plant; it can take a number of weeks before the seeds are released.
7 **CHECK** every now and then by looking inside the bag to see if the pods have dried. You can often hear them falling.

When you harvest seeds don't be greedy; leave some seed heads behind for the birds to feed on and for future plants to grow.

BELOW The Red Campion's stems hold seedpods and flowers at the same time, simultaneously self-seeding and attracting pollinators.

A Cut off the pod and place in a paper bag, pods facing down.

B Store your pod-full bags suspended in a warm, dry place.

C Check your bags regularly to see whether the pods have dried – this can vary from plant to plant.

D Once you've collected the dry seeds, place them in an airtight container and store in a cool, dry and dark place.

Separate the Seed from the Chaff

Once your seed pods/seed heads are dry, the seeds are ready to be separated from all the bits of plant debris that surround them – this is called the chaff. It can be quite tricky, and being prepared with a clear space and the right tools is a good way to start. There are a few ways of getting seeds from the pod and it depends on the plant. Wind-dispersed seeds are released from the pods by gently tapping against a bowl or some paper. Some wind-dispersed pods have chambers, which seeds will hide in and will need to be gently crushed in a sieve over a bowl; the sieve will catch the chaff and allow the seed to fall through. Clustered seed heads, like marigolds, should be pinched apart once dried.

TAKE DOWN your bags plant by plant (so as not to mix up the seeds).
LAY OUT newspaper on the table or floor.
PLACE a sieve over the bowl.
TEAR OPEN the bag, leaving the corners intact as seeds may have collected there.
REMOVE the stems and place them on the newspaper.
TIP the remaining seeds from the bag into the sieve to separate the chaff.
TWEEZER any remaining seeds out of tricky corners.
DRY the seeds for a couple of days in a paper or card container.
PLACE in a labelled airtight jar.
STORE in a cool, dry and dark place. Correct storage can lengthen the lives of seeds considerably.

YOU WILL NEED

Paper bags or newspaper

Bowls

Sieves

Tweezers

Paper/card container

Seed Companies

Seed production is a worldwide multi-billion dollar business. Most seeds are produced by large specialist growers who produce only a few crop types. The large companies sell seeds wholesale to smaller companies, who then package them into smaller packets to sell to the amateur gardener.

More recently, GM crops have been introduced into the picture. Many multinational seed companies have vested interests in this technology, since GM seed can be patented and potentially offers greater control of the market. Many farmers and gardeners have begun to react to this by reclaiming their rights to grow non-hybrid seeds for saving and swapping.

After the Haiti earthquake in 2010, Monsanto, the world's biggest seed company and market leader in selling GM seeds, donated a US$4 million 'gift' of 60,000 seed sacks. The hybrid seeds were treated with highly toxic pesticides and needed to be handled with protective gloves. The Ministry of Agriculture rejected Monsanto's offer as concerns were raised that by accepting the 'gift', small farmers would enter agreements which may have resulted in being forced to buy Monsanto's expensive seeds each year. Approximately 10,000 Haitian farmers and protesters burned the seeds on June 4 2010 for World Environment Day (www. foodsafetynews.com).

The Safe Seed Pledge

Before the rise of commercial seed giants, most practised gardeners and farmers selected and saved seeds from the healthiest plants. These were grown the following year and so on, thus strengthening the strain. This way of thinking and doing guaranteed local adaptation to pests and diseases and ensured genetic diversity. The recent uprising among farmers and ethical seed companies around the world, who believe in seed freedom and sovereignty, has germinated in to a recognised oath called 'The Safe Seed Pledge'. The pledge was initiated in 1999 by High Mowing Organic Seeds as a statement about the signers' stand against genetic modification. So far, over 70 seed companies have signed the pledge. For a list, visit www.the councilforresponsiblegenetics.org

RIGHT GM crops – a new and potentially serious threat to the diversity of our crops.

❝ We pledge that we do not knowingly buy or sell genetically engineered seeds or plants. ❞

Chapter 2

SEED SAVING

Where to Source Seeds

Sourcing seeds from your local community is ideal, because plants adapt so well to where they are growing. Seed swaps or asking your neighbours if they have any surplus seeds is a good start, but sometimes this isn't possible so shops and garden centres will be your next port of call.

However, even though they are the closest, they may not be the best places to shop, since the seeds on their shelves may come from far away, and worse, may not have been stored properly and may not have good germination rates. If you have to go to your local garden centre, find the manager and ask him about the seeds. Below are some good websites. They are usually happy to offer advice.

Sustainable Seeds USA
Having taken the 'Safe Seed Pledge', this company strives to enrich people's lives through community. It sells its own-grown heritage seeds and seeds from small organic seed farmers. In the company's own words, they are 'promoting self-sufficiency through food independence.' www.sustainableseedco.com

The Real Seed Catalogue UK
Registered with Defra, this is an online catalogue of heritage and heritage varieties of vegetable seeds grown with the home gardener and the promotion of seed saving in mind. www.realseeds.co.uk

Lunar Organics UK
How to garden following the phases of the moon, with open-pollinated, heritage, biodynamic seeds. www.lunarorganics.com

Association Kokopelli France
Certified by 'Ulase', 'Nature et Progres' and the 'Soil Association', this is a not-for-profit organisation working with European farmers and growers of open-pollinated heritage seeds 'for the liberation of seed and soil.' www.kokopelli-seeds.com

Heirloom Seeds USA
A small, family-run seed house selling seeds grown by backyard gardeners, whose families have saved the seeds for generations throughout the USA, Canada, Mexico and overseas. Their seeds meet or exceed federal standards. www.heirloomseeds.com

Magic Garden Seeds Germany
A small seed company based in Bavaria, which specialises in open-pollinated heritage, 'ethnobotanical' seeds. www.magicgardenseeds.com

TOP Organise your seeds well and swappers get exactly what they need.

MIDDLE A member of the Curcubit family, Achocha seed is said to have been grown by the ancient Inca tribe in South America as a food crop.

BOTTOM You can pass on any surplus seeds that you have purchased that are fit for swapping.

Royal Horticultural Society UK

One of the many benefits of belonging to this society is the opportunity to join their seed distribution scheme. Every year they harvest seeds from hundreds of different plant varieties from their own four gardens. They only distribute to addresses in the European Union, as well as Iceland, the UK, Norway and Switzerland. www.rhs.org.uk

What to Look Out For

Before buying seeds, consider what to grow. Choose vegetables that your family enjoys eating and some unusual ones to try out. Measure out your growing space, estimate how tall and wide the crops will be, and find out whether or not they will thrive in your soil and site.

Guidelines for Buying Seeds

The internet has a wealth of information but it's important to make sure you get your seeds from a reputable source and that they have been harvested and stored correctly. There is a risk that you might buy from a novice who sells you diseased, damaged, badly stored or dead seeds.

Before buying, ask these questions:

› **HOW HAVE THE SEEDS BEEN STORED BEFORE SALE?** If a seed packet has been sitting for months on a shelf in a hot garden centre, or in someone's damp shed, they will be very poor. Seeds are living organisms and need to be stored at the correct temperature and humidity to maintain viability.
› **WHERE ARE THEY GROWN?** Foreign-grown seed is unlikely to suit your growing conditions, and the plants may struggle in your garden as a result. Try to make sure you buy seeds of relatively local origin.
› **IS IT AN F1 HYBRID?** If you want to save seeds true to type, you must find out if the seeds are open-pollinated.

Keep records of where you got your seeds from, how many you ordered and how much they were. This information can be a useful resource for future purchases.

Shelf-Life

As soon as seeds are harvested they begin to age, and if they aren't stored properly they are at risk of dying or losing vigour. Aged seeds may be slow to germinate or they may fail to germinate at all. Sometimes they produce abnormal seedlings.

The 'shelf-life' (longevity) of seeds varies from plant to plant. Some are short lived, but most are capable of surviving for many years under the optimum storage conditions. Scientists from Kew's Millennium Seed Bank at Wakehurst Place conduct comparative seed longevity experiments where seeds are 'aged' to develop a ranking category. They have discovered that seeds with an endosperm (and so with relatively smaller embryos) from plants that grow in cool, moist environments are likely to have a shorter life than non-endospermic seeds (with relatively larger embryos) that come from warmer, drier regions.

In the autumn of 1879, Dr William James Beal, then professor of botany and forestry at Michigan Agricultural College, USA, initiated a seed viability experiment, which is the longest-running experiment on seed longevity. He prepared 20 lots and selected 50 fresh seeds from 23 different plants. The seeds were mixed with moderately moist sand and placed in uncorked pint bottles, which were buried 1m deep with the mouth slanted downwards so water couldn't accumulate around the seeds. The bottles were laid out

in rows and buried in a sandy hilltop near the College on unploughed land. Every five years a bottle was dug up, and its contents mixed with soil in seed trays and tested for germination.

After 40 years, amaranth (*Amaranthus*), germinated successfully, followed by *Oenothera*, *Brassica* and *Rumex crispus*. The fifteenth bottle was recovered on 22 April 2000 after being buried for 120 years. Twenty-three seeds of *Verbascum blattaria* and two seeds of a different *Verbascum* species germinated and produced normal plants, and a single seed of *Malva rotundifolia* germinated after six week's cold treatment. Five more bottles were left buried.

ABOVE All aspects of seed development are studied by scientists at Kew's Millennium Seed Bank.

RIGHT In an experiment, amaranth germinated from 40-year-old seed.

Tips & Techniques

Remember that seeds stored in an open container will absorb moisture from the air, promoting ageing, germination and possibly rotting.

WHEN IS A SEED DRY ENOUGH TO STORE?
Farmers mix equal amounts of salt with seeds in a glass jar, shake it and leave it for 20 minutes. If the seeds are still wet, the salt absorbs their moisture and will stick to the sides of the jar. Scientists at Kew's Millennium Seed Bank at Wakehurst Place use digital hygrometers, which measure the air surrounding the seed after 30 minutes in a sealed chamber. It gives an accurate reading of the equilibrium relative humidity (eRH). For short-term storage, a reading of below 70% eRH is acceptable, but 15% eRH is recommended for long-term storage, preferably under cold conditions. Some cheaper alternatives, such as self-indicating silica gel and moisture-indicating strips, are available online or from specialist suppliers.

TEMPERATURE The shelf life of seeds decreases if temperatures are high. Ideally the storage temperatures should be minus 20°C. The Millennium Seed Bank suggests that for every 5°C reduction in temperature, seed longevity will double.

AMBIENT DRYING In many countries the sun is used to dry out seeds, which are traditionally laid out on a tarpaulin and shuffled occasionally. Alternatively, you can dry seeds in porous bags in crates, raised off the floor to improve air circulation. For small-scale seed saving, the humble paper bag is perfectly acceptable.

RICE DRY Rice draws the moisture from your seeds. Bake the rice for 45 minutes, and while still hot pour into a large glass jar and screw the lid on, waiting for the rice to cool. Add your seeds to a porous bag, for example a paper bag or one made from some old cotton socks, tie shut and place on top of the rice. Tighten the lid and store in a cool, dry, dark place for two weeks. After this, the seeds should be dry enough to be stored in an airtight container.

POWDERED MILK If you often open the container to use your seeds, moisture could seep in. As a back-up to keep your seeds dry, you can make a pocket from a piece of kitchen towel and fill it with powdered milk. Secure the pocket shut with a paperclip and leave it in your seed container for up to six months.

Seed Saving Techniques

These techniques will help to ensure the seeds you save are 'true', which means that they have not cross-pollinated with others in their species or wild relatives, resulting in physical deformities. It is also important that seeds are dried and stored in such a way as to ensure successful germination.

Isolation & Caging

These are ways of preventing cross-pollination.

Isolation

The isolation distance must be far enough to prevent pollen from being carried by the wind and visiting insects – it varies from species to species. For example, aubergines can be isolated by just 15.5m, whereas beetroot needs at least 5 miles. Isolating varieties may be a difficult thing to accomplish if you live in a built-up area and your neighbour is growing plants of the same species. Consequently, isolation isn't very effective for urban areas, unless you are growing uncommon plants.

Time Isolation

Annual varieties can be isolated by time. Separate the flowering periods by planting two varieties with different maturity rates, such as an early crop and a late crop. Plant the first crop as early as possible, and just before the first crop flowers you can sow the next variety. This works well with crops such as coriander, sunflower, corn and lettuce.

Bagging Flowers

Bagging is a method used for self-pollinating plants, such as tomatoes and aubergines, but excluding corn. By covering flowers with porous bags made from spun polyester, you are creating a barrier so the insects can't get in. Tie the bags around individual flower heads or groups. Make sure there are no gaps around the stems for insects to crawl into. Shake the plants occasionally to disperse the pollen from flower to flower, and when the fruits have formed, remove the bag and mark the plant as being the one from which you can save seeds.

Caging

Pollination cages can be used for both self- and insect-pollinated plants. Cover them with spun polyester or fine net curtains. These net cages need to have good air flow, to allow in water and light and to keep insects out. Low-growing crops can be caged by using bendy poles or wire semi circles pushed into the ground. Bigger crop cages can be made from wood or plastic pipes. Make sure the fabric is buried under the soil to prevent any insect squatters!

TOP Wild carrot is a common weed that will cross-pollinate with your vegetable carrots.

MIDDLE Winnowing seperates the seeds from the chaff by throwing them up and allowing the air current to blow away from the lighter particles.

BOTTOM Rubbing material through a screen or sieve first helps to get rid of the tricky fluffy bits and the big bits.

Introducing pollinators into your cages is essential for insect-pollinated plants. Honey bees can be lured inside by placing a plate of honey beside the cage. Alternatively, you can buy maggots from an angling shop, allow them to turn into casters in a warm place, then put them in your cage to turn into flies.

Alternate Day Caging

You can grow a number of different varieties of the same plant in your garden. Remove the cage from one variety each day (replace the cage in the evening) to allow it to be naturally pollinated by insects without the risk of crossing with the other caged varieties.

Hand-pollination

This allows you to 'hand' transfer pollen from flower to flower to prevent cross-pollination (see page 19).

Threshing & Winnowing

These are dry seed-processing techniques that separate the seeds from the chaff.

Threshing

The seeds are released from their coverings by rubbing, beating or flailing. Whole seed heads can be placed in a pillowcase and gently trampled. Smaller seeds can be carefully mashed between two boards.

Winnowing

Used to separate the smaller chaff from seeds, one method is to toss seeds from a basket. This allows the wind to separate the lighter debris from the heavier seed. However, a sudden gust of wind could take your whole seed collection with it. An alternative to wind is to use a household fan or an old hairdryer with the heating element taken out. Cover the area you are winnowing with a sheet to catch any stray seeds.

Dry Seeds & Wet Seeds

Different seeds require different harvesting and saving techniques. Some plants set seed after one growing season but others may need more planning like biennial vegetables such as carrots and onions. These need two growing seasons and a period of cold before they set seed. Some seeds are released from the plant only when the seed head or pod has dried, and these include plants such as sweetcorn, beans and carrots. Other seeds are contained within a fleshy fruit, like tomatoes and courgettes; and will need extraction methods such as scraping out and soaking, and for germinating in the short term, they may also need fermenting.

Dry Seeds

Dry seeds are not hidden within a fleshy fruit. Usually when the flower has died, the petals fall away or go brown, and the seed head or pod will form and swell. Collect the seeds on a sunny day when they feel dry and before the seed head breaks open or is eaten by birds.

Allocate a paper bag or pillowcase and label it with the plant you are collecting from so as not to mix up the seeds.

Cut off the seed heads or pods with up to 20cm of stem, and place them head down in the bag. Tie the bag closed around the stems and hang it up in a well-ventilated, dry place indoors for up to three weeks.

It is relatively simple with dry seeds, to separate the seeds from the chaff, since the seeds tend to be released as the seed head dries. Threshing and winnowing may be required (see page 39).

Wet Seeds

Wet seeds such as, cucumber and squash, are embedded within a fleshy fruit and need to be separated from the flesh before you dry them. Some fruits, such as courgette, are deliberately harvested when young for consumption, but need to be grown on for a further several weeks before the seeds become ripe for collection.

ABOVE Remember you should only ever store seeds when they are completely dry.

RIGHT Wet seeds need to be scraped out of the fruit. Sieve and wash seeds thoroughly. Dry seeds completely before storing.

Separating the Seeds from the Pulp

Large fruits like pumpkin are usually chopped open and the seeds are scraped out with a spoon. They are then sieved and pulled apart under a running tap.

Seeds from small fruits like tomatoes need to be lightly mashed out with the juices into a bowl and washed and sieved repeatedly until they are clean.

Wet seeds will stick to porous things such as paper, so they should be laid out evenly over a labelled ceramic plate or drying screen for a number of days in a dry spot. Shuffle and turn the seeds occasionally to prevent them from sticking to each other or rotting.

When the seeds are properly dry, store them in a labelled, airtight container.

For germinating in the short term, some wet seeds can undergo the fermenting process (see page 43).

TIP Remember it is important to wait for the seeds to mature on the plant

"ALL THE FLOWERS OF TOMORROW ARE IN THE SEEDS OF YESTERDAY."

Italian Proverb

before you harvest them. This applies just as much to wet seeds as it does to dry seeds. For 'wet seeds' allow the fruit to go over ripe and for 'dry seeds' the seeds will usually change colour, harden and loosen on the seed head.

Fermentation

Fermentation occurs as a natural process in the garden as the fruits fall to the ground and rot, or are passed through the digestive system of an animal. Fermentation kills off any seed-borne diseases that can affect the next generation of plants and improves the ability to sprout by degrading growth inhibitors. Only ferment seeds that you are likely to germinate in the short term, within five years. The fermentation process is not suitable if you don't want to store seeds for longer than this because you don't want to degrade the growth inhibitors.

The fermentation process can easily be mimicked in the kitchen. Scoop out the seeds and pulp into a jar and fill it with double the amount of water. Stir vigorously and store the mixture in a warm place at 30°C for up to three days until you see white bubbling on the surface of the mixture. After a day of bubbling, pour the brew into a bowl of water and gently separate the seeds from the pulp with your fingers. Live seeds will sink to the bottom of the bowl. Rinse and sieve several times, then place the seeds on a plate in a cool, dry place for several days before storing them in an airtight container.

It is questionable as to whether the fermentation process helps or hinders seeds that you want to store in the long term, because the growth inhibitors keep the seed dormant and are likely to degrade over time in long-term storage anyway. I suggest that during the cleaning process, you put a batch aside without fermentation, so that you can hedge your bets.

ABOVE It may not look pretty, but fermentation stops disease passing from one generation to the next. Why not try fermentation at home before storing, and see if it makes a difference to the shelf-life of your seeds.

Chapter 3

SEED SWAPPING

What is Seed Swapping?

Seed swapping is about engaging with your community, sharing seeds with friends, neighbours and relatives, and exchanging knowledge and ideas. At the same time, this fascinating activity makes it more likely that the genetic integrity of a plant is preserved and passed on.

This book covers the what, who, how and whys of seed swapping and seed saving. It advises where to start and how to get involved with the worldwide horticultural campaign to 'save our seeds'. The work of seed activist individuals and groups is highlighted with inspirational tips and tales, and there is insight into the practices of major seed companies and how this has affected seed diversity and how 'seed breeding' affects the future of plants. The work of seed collections and seed banks is explored, and advice is given on how to collect, clean, store, preserve and raise seeds. The second part of the book contains an extensive plant directory, which is full of advice on how to grow plants from 'seed to seed'.

I have enjoyed seed saving for all of my gardening career. For me, it is one of the most exciting of garden tasks, and it represents the end of the season, a time for reflection. I enjoy the whole seed-saving process and sharing my garden's seed bounty with my friends and the community.

Why Swap Seeds?

Seed swapping is a means of exchanging surplus seeds as a goodwill gesture, and usually takes place at organised gatherings for novice and seasoned gardeners. Participants trade their seeds and knowledge in a local community hall or someone's house, or even via a 'round robin'.

With the increase in the cost of living, seed swapping is a great way of becoming more self sufficient in the ornamental garden as well as the fruit and vegetable garden. Saving and swapping seeds has a wealth of benefits, from financial savings through to maintaining food security and protecting biodiversity, rare species and seed genetics. It also helps to disseminate the practices and ideas of other cultures, which may be linked to particular plant species and their varieties. Seeds have the ability to travel great distances, and those with the greatest cultural significance tend to get transported by people as they move around the globe.

Swapping seeds expands plant variety in a 'swapper's' garden. At seed swaps, a wealth of local knowledge and wisdom can be exchanged, about what works – or doesn't work – in your microclimate, and you are likely to discover new and exciting plants. Keeping things 'local' helps the community become independent from seed manufacturers who tend to have control over the availability and variety of seeds. Although seed saving has

> **"** *Seeds are, in a sense, suitcases in which people can transport their cultures with them... Many families have brought their favourite seeds on tremendous journeys.* **"**
>
> **Mike Szuberla**
> ORGANISER OF A SEED SWAP IN TOLEDO, OHIO

LEFT Collecting seeds from my garden – not only great fun but meaningful too.

ABOVE Seed swap events are increasingly popular internationally, and provide a great opportunity for enthusiasts to source new seeds and mix with like-minded people.

a long history, global events like Seedy Saturday and Seedy Sunday only began in 1990. Communities could come together to share seeds and gardening stories. Seasoned seed-swap gardeners incorporate collecting seeds into their gardening routine specifi cally for seed-swapping events, and the ever-increasing popularity of these occasions has gained the interest of keen novices too.

Getting Involved

Today, seed-swapping events happen all across the world, and if you are interested, it isn't hard to find one, whether it be your local community hall, allotments or even online.

Attending a Seed Swap

The internet has masses of information on seed-swapping events. It is worth asking at your local allotments too. It is best to stay in your area as you are more likely to fi nd plants that are happy growing in the conditions provided by your local climate.

Start a 'Round Robin' Seed Swap

Swap seeds without having to pay for the hire of a venue by starting a seed-swapping chain.

> › **COLLECT NAMES** of the willing participants and provide the fi nal list of names to everyone involved.
> › **SEND A PACKAGE** filled with your surplus seeds to the next person on the list.
> › **THE NEXT PERSON** will then take one packet of seeds from the package and replace them with some more seeds.
> › **THE PACKAGE** is sent to the next person on the list, who removes and replaces as above.
> › **THE CHAIN CARRIES ON** until the last person on the list posts the package (which should now contain a completely different combination of seeds) backto the original organiser.

Seed Circles

A seed circle is where a group of friends or allotment buddies each sign up to save seeds from one or two sorts of plant. At

ABOVE Go along and have a rummage! You never know what you may find.

RIGHT Check your seeds thoroughly before a swap to make sure they are fresh and healthy.

FAR RIGHT Write any useful information about the seeds on the front of the envelope. Seal your seeds in small labelled envelopes or handmade customised seed packets.

the end of the growing season, each person saves what they need and arranges to share or exchange their surplus seeds with the rest of the circle.

Organising a seed circle is really easy. This is what you need to get started:

> **AN ORGANISER** – you!
> **A DEDICATED GROUP** – this can be small or large.
> **A SIGN-UP FORM** – to collect everyone's contact details.
> **AN INFORMATION SHEET** – to include important tips, such as how to save and store seeds, and your contact details.
> **A SPARE MOMENT** – to check in on everyone's progress.
> **GOOD QUALITY, FRESH, NON-HYBRID SEEDS** – to start your circle.

Etiquette

There are a few things to bear in mind before you go to a seed swap.

1 **PLANT CHOICE** Bring non-invasive, open-pollinated seeds (see page 22).

2 **SEED VIABILITY** Vegetable seeds should be no older than three years, unless they have been properly dried and stored. As they age, seeds are less likely to germinate successfully.

3 **PACKAGING & LABELLING** It can be fun making your own seed packets and labels. Make sure you include important information such as the date, plant name (common and scientific), eventual height and spread, and any growing tips.

4 **ORGANISATION** For ease of exchange, display seeds in boxes categorised by plant type, such as tree, climber or vegetable.

TIP Start with fruits, vegetables or flowers that you know you like. Perhaps discuss with the group what seeds everybody would like to eventually have.

Seed Activism

Seed activism is a global uprising of farmers and gardeners who believe in the freedom to save and share seeds without having to purchase them from major seed companies. Some seed companies engineer plant varieties that produce unviable seeds. Such seeds cannot be grown on, so the gardener is forced to buy, buy and buy again.

Ideas, Activities & Events

Seedy Sunday Brighton
A grass roots event inspired by the anti-genetic engineering Seedy Saturday event in Canada. Seedy Sunday is currently the biggest seed swap in the UK. It has been running for 11 years and campaigns against buying seeds from companies selling F1 hybrid seeds (see pages 22–23), which are incapable of producing worthy seeds to use the next year. The Seedy Sunday (www.seedysunday.org) event in Brighton takes place every February and has up to 2,000 seed activists attending workshops and talks, and swapping seeds.

Seedbombs
We can't talk about seed activism without mentioning seedbombing! This is a growing phenomenon whereby 'guerrilla' gardeners beautify urban wasteland with balls of native wildflowers mixed with water, earth and clay.

Inspiration
Dr Vandana Shiva, founder of Navdanya is a scientist, environmentalist, activist, visionary and passionate campaigner for

" Seeds are the first link in the food chain as well as being the storage place for culture and history and we have the right to save and share them."

Dr Vandana Shiva
(WWW.NAVDANYA.ORG)

seed sovereignty. She campaigns against any technology practised by large seed companies who seek to use genetically modified plants to produce sterile or unviable seeds, which prevents farmers from saving seeds to plant the following season. Dr Shiva believes that free seed exchange among farmers and growers is the basis of maintaining biodiversity, food security and centuries of stories and wisdom. Her work has inspired the initiation of seed libraries and seed swapping across the globe.

Seed Libraries

These are lending institutions as opposed to seed banks, which primarily save and preserve seeds. They have been initiated by community groups and individuals who are against the control of our seed supply by seed companies, and they believe in seed sovereignty and protecting biodiversity.

Seed libraries follow the model of lending libraries for books, in that seeds are 'checked out' with the intention of growing them. In turn, the seeds that grow from them are returned to the library.

Start a Seed Library

If you are tempted to start your own seed library, try these basic steps below.

1 **FIND A GROUP OF ENTHUSIASTS TO RUN THE LIBRARY** Look online and in community spaces.
2 **FIND A VENUE** A well-visited community space, such as a library or community hall, would make a good meeting place.
3 **FIND MATERIALS** An unwanted wine cooler or chilled vending machine could be used for keeping well-dried seeds cool and easily accessible.
4 **FUNDRAISE** Write to local, non-hybrid seed companies explaining your cause and ask for donations.
5 **ADVERTISE** Advertise a seed collection

point, asking for seed donations. Give strict guidelines such as to which seeds will be accepted and which will not be accepted.
6 **GET EQUIPPED** Assemble a few stationery items such as envelopes, rubber stamps for checking seeds in and out, and labels. Use a computer to set up a borrower's database.
7 **FIND A SIGN** Use recycled materials to create an eye-catching seed-saving library sign.
8 **FIND YOUR BORROWERS** Create a media buzz using flyers, posters, social media and a website.

TOP Seedbombs – seeds mixed with clay, earth and water – are a great way of planting-up otherwise barren urban landscapes.

ABOVE Seedy Sunday in Brighton attracts seed activists from all over the world.

FAR LEFT The inspirational Vandana Shiva, a passionate advocate of seed saving. Shiva received the Right Livelihood Award in 1993.

Early Seed Swaps

The knowledge accumulated by ethnobotanists enables us to see how our forefathers used plants for culinary and medicinal purposes. Plants were exchanged when travellers would visit or migrate to different countries, and these exchanges fundamentally changed each culture. When European explorers travelled to the Americas in 1492, crops such as wheat, onions, garlic and wine grapes, and herbs such as coriander and parsley were taken with them. Squash, beans, corn and potatoes were brought back to Europe. Some seeds were intentionally exchanged and some were unknowingly transported, hidden in nooks and crannies of the ships and dispersed by the elements on arrival. This process carried the risk of transporting alien species that could affect native plants and crops by being invasive and introducing pests and diseases. More positively, it means that seeds that once belonged to a particular country now belong to the world.

Foods of Your Culture

Cultural foods are meaningful. Their smell and taste evoke memories, and some travellers will take the traditional foods of their region on long journeys because they are vital to their diets and have physical and spiritual significance. The demand for traditional vegetables, herbs and spices has inspired multicultural street markets and some convenience stores to stock unusual and exciting grains, fruits, vegetables and spices. Those who have emigrated can therefore continue to cook the food of their culture using traditional herbs and spices.

ABOVE Just like people, seeds and foods pass from one culture to another, enriching the lives and diets of people as they travel. What was once exotic, becomes commonplace.

"THE EARTH IS WHAT WE
ALL HAVE IN COMMON."

Wendell Berry

Saving by Saving

Money is tight and times are tough, so why not cut some of your costs by saving and swapping seeds? Using your seeds as currency to gain further seeds can save considerably, and a successful seed circle will mean you'll never have to buy seeds again!

Seed Circle Maths

> 15 savers of two different vegetables results in 30 packets of seeds each.
> An average packet of seeds costs £2.50, so that's a saving of £75 per year.
> Store them and grow two different vegetables next season.
> By the third year of your seed circle, everyone will have 90 packets of different seeds.

Time Saving & Stocking Up

The benefits of saving and swapping seeds are not only financial, they may also help you save time. If someone else grows the plant first time round, you will get the benefit of his or her experience. You can stock up on time-saving growing tips and ways to avoid potential disasters. The best thing about community seed sharing and swapping is that any experience earned will be specific to your local growing conditions, and the chance to pool all the combined knowledge from your community is invaluable to your gardening experience.

Seed swapping is an 'exchange' and an opportunity to pass on any helpful tips and techniques about the seeds you swap. These should be passed on, either on the seed packet or on an attached note.

TIP Remember to only use open-pollinated seeds for your seed circle so they will produce plants with viable seeds to pass on that are true to type.

Environmental Benefits

Community

Seed swapping strengthens community links. It's a great way of making new friends and there will probably be lots of interesting conversations you can earwig or join in with. At seed swaps there are often talks and workshops on related subjects, such as beekeeping, wildflowers, rare plants, bio-diversity and even how to cook with your home produce.

Food Diversity

Conserving seeds is conserving food diversity and a diverse range of crops. It took 10,000 years to develop the agricultural diversity we enjoy today, and this is being threatened by global food industries whose single aim is profit. As a result, we have hyper-productive, hyper-durable plant varieties in place of organically grown, open-pollinated plants.

Food diversity is plummeting into a world of mono-cropping. The seed-saving community is seed activism at its best, a worldwide group effort to preserve plant diversity.

Wildlife

Saving seeds saves species. Plant diversity supports wildlife diversity, and together they create a healthy ecosystem that is fundamental to the existence of all living things. The US Fish and Wildlife Service estimates that losing one plant species can trigger the loss of up to 30 other insect, plant and animal species.

Food Security

Seed savers sow the seeds of food security by growing and eating their own produce. This means that their produce doesn't have far to travel from plot to plate, and gardeners have control over which foods they grow, to suit their culture and diet. Being able to save seeds from your own garden secures a food supply for you, for future generations of your family, and for the community with which you seed swap.

LEFT Organise your seeds so that they are easy to look through.

ABOVE Home-grown heritage vegetables are just one way in which individuals are helping to preserve food diversity.

Banking on Seed Collections

Are we banking on the fact that our food reserves will always be here?

Pioneers like Nikolai Vavilov paved the way for the contemporary seed banks and collections. The son of a merchant in Moscow, he was born in 1887. He became a prominent Soviet botanist, geneticist and one of the world's first scientists to raise international awareness of the need to conserve plants.

The poor rural village in which he grew up was plagued by crop failure and rationing. This fuelled his passion for ending famine and his whole life was devoted to studying and improving the cereal crops that sustain the global population. He studied at Moscow Agricultural Institute where he wrote his dissertation on snails and plant pests. He studied plant immunity in Europe and organised botanical-agronomic expeditions to collect seeds from around the globe, which were stored in a seed bank in Leningrad. The resulting seed bank eventually contained 400,000 seeds, roots and fruits. It was, at the time, the world's largest collection of plant seeds.

The 900-day siege of Leningrad (8 September 1941 to 27 January 1944) posed a threat to the seed bank. Convinced that Hitler had his sights set on the seeds so he could control the world's food supply, Vavilov's scientists boxed up a range of seeds and hid them in the basement. They guarded them in shifts, and although facing starvation, they refused to eat any of the seeds as they belonged to the 'future'. Sadly, 12 of the self-appointed seed guardians died of malnourishment whilst protecting the seeds.

On 6 August 1940, Vavilov was arrested for allegedly destroying Soviet agriculture. He died of malnutrition in a prison in 1943, but not before giving over 100 hours of science lectures. The collection of 200,000 seeds from the Soviet Union and from abroad was seized by a German SS squad in 1943 and partially relocated to the SS Institute for Plant Genetics, which had been set up at Lannach Castle in Austria. The seeds are still missing but it is believed that some of them ended up in Sweden, England and Argentina.

ABOVE LEFT Nikolai Vavilov (1887–1943), a prominent Soviet scientist and one of the first plant conservationists.

ABOVE Soviet farmers in 1929, a year in which many poor rural areas suffered from crop failure.

RIGHT The largest of the world's seeds, from the coco-de-mer palm, can grow up to 30cm long.

Seed Diversity

Seed-bearing plants are grouped into two different divisions: angiosperms and gymnosperms. Angiosperms have 'enclosed seeds', in that the seeds are protected inside an ovary. Angiosperms are flowering plants and are the largest group of plants, making up 90% of all plant species. The seeds are produced in a fruit, which often helps with seed dispersal. Flowers have been the major success of angiosperms, as it enables them to employ the activities of animal visitors to help with their breeding. Gymnosperms have 'naked seeds', in that the seeds lie uncovered on the surface of a scale. The largest group of gymnosperms are the conifers, which include pines, cedars, spruces, gingkos and fir trees.

The World's Smallest Seed
This seed is borne by certain epiphytic (tree-dwelling) orchids that grow in tropical rainforests. They produce dust-like seeds that are 85 micrometres long.

The World's Largest Seed
This seed is produced by the coco-de-mer palm, *Lodoicea maldivica*. The seeds grow up to 30cm long and can weigh 18kg!

Crop Diversity

The loss of crop diversity and the vulnerability of the world's seed collections has been a concern among scientists for many years. Worldwide agriculture relies on approximately 150 crops, and each crop has a vast range of forms, habits and tolerances; however, the wild relatives of crops are under threat from the effects of climate change and so the need to conserve our seed diversity has never been greater. Seed saving is one way to preserve seed and plant diversity for future generations.

"WE DON'T INHERIT THE EARTH FROM OUR ANCESTORS, WE BORROW IT FROM OUR CHILDREN."

Native American proverb

Seed Swapping Organisations

The National Gardening Association
Vermont, USA
Provides for two-way swaps as well as a forum to post your 'wish lists' and lists of seeds to trade. www.garden.org/seedswap

Native Seeds Arizona, USA
The regional seed bank and leader of the heritage seed movement, promoting ancient crops and their wild relatives by gathering, documenting, safeguarding, and distributing to farming/gardening communities. Their mantra is 'returning the seeds of grandparents to people who seek them, and to make available to everyone this wondrous gift, the delicious joy of seeds.' www.nativeseeds.org

Pelti Alternative Community Greece
Founded by Panagiotis Sainatoudis and located in the remote valley of Mesohori. Peliti collects, distributes and aims to preserve Greece's traditional varieties. The community has celebrated its 12th annual 'Pan-Hellenic Festival for the exchange of local variety seed'. www.peliti.gr

The Seed Ambassadors Project
Oregon, USA
Initiated by a group of 'seed stewards', who are devoted to seeds. They travel around Europe learning about seeds and exchanging knowledge to bring back to their farm, where they grow, save and swap heritage seeds.
www.seedambassadors.org

Seeds of Diversity Canada
A volunteer organisation active in conserving the biodiversity and traditional knowledge of food crops and garden plants. www.seeds.ca/en.php

Seed Savers Exchange Iowa, USA
Known for their seed swapping catalogue of thousands of vegetable and fruits.
www.seedsavers.org

Southern Seed Legacy Project
Texas, USA
Strives to preserve plant genetic diversity and cultural knowledge in South America by supporting local seed saving and exchange networks as well as local conservation. www.pacs.unt. edu/southernseedlegacy

The Global Crop Diversity Trust Italy
Aims to ensure the worldwide conservation and availability of crop diversity for food security.
www.croptrust.org

Primal Seeds UK
An information network promoting seed saving and swapping, and supporting grassroots movements around the world.
www.primalseeds.org

International Seedsaving Institute
Idaho, USA
A not-for-profit, educational organisation focusing on helping people become self-reliant. www.seedsave.org

Seedswaps
A free seed trading website
www.seedswaps.com

Dyfi Valley Seed Savers Wales, UK
A not-for-profit seed-swapping and seed-saving organisation.
www.dyfi valleyseedsavers.org.uk

Chapter 4

AN INTRO TO
SEEDBOMBING

What is a Seedbomb?

When I tell people I make seedbombs, they look puzzled and ask, 'What is a seedbomb?'. They think they are edible (some fancy new superfood) or a cosmetic product. Rarely do people think they are horticultural. I smile and begin a well-rehearsed explanation.

Firstly, they are **NOT EXPLOSIVE OR EDIBLE!** A seedbomb is a little ball made up of a combination of compost, clay and seeds.

'What is it For?'
The compost and clay act as a carrier for the seeds so they can be launched over walls or fences and into inaccessible areas such as wasteland or railways.

'But What is the Point? Why Can't You Just Throw Seeds Loose?'
Most seeds are very light and there is risk of them being blown away by the wind, making them unsuitable for launching long distances.

'How Do I Make Them?'
There are various ways of making seedbombs. You need to find a carrier for the seeds. My method uses natural ingredients – compost and clay. The compost offers nutrients for the seeds to germinate and grow strong during their

infancy and the clay binds the seedbomb, making it hard enough not to break when it hits the ground.

'How Do They Work?'
After about 3 weeks the first seedlings work their way through the seedbomb and root into the ground below. The seedlings will then grow into mature plants and face whatever conditions Mother Nature has in store for them. As they grow, more seeds germinate and the seedbomb begins to dissolve. This can take days, weeks or months – it depends on the quantity of rainfall. Seeds will remain dormant until their environmental needs are met with these factors: water, correct temperature and a good position to grow in.

There is a sense of unpredictability with seedbombing. Its random nature is what attracts people, the magic of waiting to see if this strange little ball will grow ... if it actually works.

RIGHT
1 Mix your seeds.
2 Roll your ball.
3 Launch your seedbomb.
4 Watch it flourish!

The Beauty of Seedbombing

Here you have in the palm of your hand a little revolution, something that can change the face of the earth, something that contains the early stages of a field of wildflowers, edible crops or a herb garden.

You can use seeds of one plant for your seedbombs or combinations of compatible seeds. This is called 'companion planting', where you use plants that grow well together and assist each other in a number of ways, such as pollination, deterring pests and soil conditioning. With a little help from Mother Nature, something as small as a seedbomb has the potential to improve the natural structure of an area in one fell swoop.

Sensible Seedbombing

A seedbomb is a little ball of life and comes with a responsibility to choose your plants and be used in the correct way.

You have to consider not only the environment where you choose to launch your seedbomb, but also the welfare of the plant. It is your job as a gardener/seedbomber to make sure the seeds get a good chance of germinating and have a good probability of reaching infancy and – even better – maturing into plants that flower and fruit and connect the ends of the circle of growth.

Launch Checklist

› Launch them at the right time of year so the right temperature is achieved
› Check the weather forecast – rain is good!
› Right plant, right place **AND AWAY WE GO**!

The seeds may germinate next week or next spring or not at all. But we still want to try it!

OPPOSITE Launch your seedbomb into desolate areas or wastelands and watch as nature begins to decorate!

ABOVE Small but powerful, they have the potential to improve an area.

Why Are They Used?

Seedbombing is another form of seed dispersal, a human intervention into what is already happening in nature anyway. It is an efficient way of deliberately dispersing seeds, but trying to work in harmony with nature, too, by being considerate of wildlife and natural habitats.

Seedbombs are seeds wrapped up in a blanket of earth, which acts as a carrier for the seeds and enables them to be launched in areas that are physically challenging to access, like fenced-off wasteland or motorway banks. Because of their size and strength they can simply be thrown over the fences or out of car, train or bus windows. They provide the accuracy needed to get the plants to where you want them to grow. It does help if your aim is good though!

The risk of damage to the seeds is minimized because the blanket of earth offers protection from harsh weather conditions and seedeaters such as mice and birds.

Apart from the fact that they are really good fun to make, they actually work and it's so exciting when you see the first shoot come through!

Like leaving a trail of breadcrumbs or petals, seedbombing is a kind of footprint, a marker for your journeys.

Where to Launch Seedbombs

Seedbombs can be launched anywhere as long as there is soil beneath them. Their versatility is part of their charm.

› They can be used in home gardens, window boxes or the veggie patch.
› Allotments – edible plants or wildflowers to attract bees to pollinate food crops.
› Launch them in alleyways and path networks around your local area.
› They can be used to create an explosion of colour on urban green roofs, on sheds or on outbuildings.
› Seedbombs are just perfect for throwing responsibly out of train, car and bus windows; they make journeys for future travellers much more attractive.
› By the side of the road, central reservations and roundabouts, railways and urban tree pits.
› Unmaintained areas, so that the seedbombs can grow undisturbed.
› Next time you see a foxglove growing by a set of traffic lights, you'll know a guerrilla gardener has been there!

RIGHT Seedbombs allow the accuracy needed for distance sowing.

A Seedbomb History

If something has been used effectively throughout time, it is given validity; you know it has been tried, tested and perfected. When it comes to seedbombs, one man has done just that. Masanobu Fukuoka incorporated his ancestral gardening techniques into his own farming methods and, in so doing, started a revolution.

Seedbombs are an ancient Japanese practice called *Tsuchi Dango*, meaning 'Earth Dumpling' (because they are made from earth). They were reintroduced in 1938 by the Japanese microbiologist/ farmer and philosopher Masanobu Fukuoka (1913–2008), author of *The One Straw Revolution*. Fukuoka led the way into the world of sustainable agriculture by initiating 'natural farming'. His methods were simple and produced no pollution. His technique used no machines or chemicals and almost no weeding.

Seedbombing was part of Fukuoka's annual farming regime. He believed that Mother Nature takes care of the seeds we sow and decides which crops to provide us with, like a process of natural selection, because ultimately nature decides what will grow and when germination will occur, be that in 7 days or several seasons away.

Fukuoka grew vegetables like wild plants – he called it 'semi wild'. He seedbombed on riverbanks, roadsides and wasteland and allowed them to 'grow up' with the weeds. He believed that vegetables grown in this way – including Japanese radish, carrots, burdock, onions and turnips – are stronger than most people think.

He'd add clover to his vegetable mixes because it acted as a living mulch and conditioned the soil.

ABOVE Fukuoka's methods were simple and non-invasive.

LEFT Fukuoka's approach to sustainable agriculture has inspired generations.

TOP Barley crop with clover, weeds and whatever else nature has in store!

LEFT Fukuoka used no machines or chemicals in his farming methods.

Projects

Where land has been intensively farmed by modern methods, the natural fertility is destroyed. Fukuoka used clover seedbombs to rehabilitate natural fertility on dead land so that food crops could be grown successfully again.

In 1998, hundreds of locals in Arnissa, Greece – families, schoolchildren, ministers, farmers, journalists – were inspired by Fukuoka's work to partake in launching tons of seedbombs over 10,000 hectares of desolate land damaged by human activity. The seeds were donated by the Ministry of Agriculture and the National Institute of Agrarian Research.

Greening Deserts with Seedbombs

Fukuoka encouraged people to collect seeds and instigated a movement for desert-greening with seedbombs. He successfully 'greened up' land all over the world, including Greece, India and the Americas.

Through his works, land has come 'alive' again, with plants and wildlife and food for the people.

❝ *Seedbombs are a small universe in themselves.* ❞

Masanobu Fukuoka

Seedbomb Benefits

Seedbombs are full of potential wrapped up in a pocket-sized ball of mud! They can make ugly, forgotten land beautiful and useful again; restore plant and wildlife populations; nourish and feed the soil, people and animals; bring communities together, educate and – importantly – bring joy.

Nature

As seen with Fukuoka's work, there are countless benefits to using the seedbomb method for planting. They are successfully used to grow food crops and meadowland and replant areas that have suffered from drought or forest fire damage, as well as being suitable for small-scale gardens and allotments.

Seedbombs help to create vegetation in areas where it is absent or sparse due to the land being neglected. They present the prospect of attracting wildlife such as bees, birds and butterflies into our urban environment, making them available to pollinate our city flowers and food crops and help the production of fruit and seed.

Seedbombs can be used to repopulate an area with diminishing numbers of wild flowers, which in turn will attract wildlife that may, too, be diminishing.

Urban Environment

On an aesthetic level, the plants provide colour and character to otherwise unattractive sites that are usually broken into and could be littered with rubbish and the classic shopping trolleys and broken glass. Areas such as this are in danger of fostering feelings of apathy, an 'Oh, what's the point, the place is a mess anyway' attitude.

Some sites stay undeveloped for a number of years and become part of the personality of the area; numerous people will walk past these places every day and not even notice the potential. Desolate spaces may be used by people acting undesirably and are often a location for fly-tipping. Unfortunately, this kind of activity could be a danger to the public because the fences get pulled down, leaving these spaces open to adventuring children.

Often no one wants to claim responsibility and implement a clear-up because ownership of the land could be a grey area, while some sites are pending construction. Guerrilla gardeners target areas like these as potential sites to glam up with donated plants and recycled, reclaimed and reused objects.

TOP An inaccessible eyesore can be transformed into a thing of beauty.

BOTTOM As well as being fun, seedbombing can bring people together with an aim to beautify an area.

The Intentional Seedbomb

Historically, seedbombs were made with natural materials, but the guerrilla gardening movement has highlighted their usefulness and people have started developing their own vessels for carrying seeds. As environmental awareness spreads, people are beginning to take action through the medium of plants.

Seedbombing is an effective way of causing real change; they can be made very easily, stored efficiently, and some have a long shelf life. And there are endless ways to launch them.

Aerial Seedbombing

There are some very sophisticated modern seedbomb designs resembling NASA-type capsules or military missiles. These are designed for long-distance launching and used for purposes such as aerial reforestation to combat or replenish areas that have suffered desertification. The capsules may contain seeds or seedlings, soil, nutrients, fertilizer and other materials that will help the plants' survival. The biodegradable casing protects the plants on impact with the ground and then disintegrates to let the roots emerge.

Some seedbombs have been designed with the military in mind for the distribution, not only for the irony but because they are professionals at launching bombs. They have the people power, the skills and the technology for tracking weather conditions and wind speed to ensure the best possible accuracy.

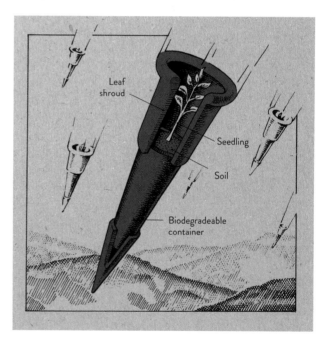

Leaf shroud

Seedling

Soil

Biodegradeable container

" The skies could be filled with military planes dropping seedbombs instead of missiles. "

One large plane could drop up to 100,000 seeds in one flight – around a million trees in just one day. Even if a certain percentage of those dropped is unsuccessful that is still a lot of trees!

In 1997, Moshe Alamaro, an Israeli former aeronautical engineer, is known to have been working on a project to drop one-year-old tree seedlings in biodegradable open-topped cones from aircraft in order to reach previously inaccessible areas such as war-torn battlefields, deserts and slopes.

Travelling at 200mph, the cones would embed themselves in the soil and decompose before the seedlings took root.

There is little information about the success of projects like this and some are still in the design process, but even the fact that people are thinking of using seedbombs as an effective replanting process on such a grand scale validates just how ingenuous they actually are.

Railway Seedbombing

I met a train driver who had decided to enhance his route by throwing foxglove seeds out of the window. Now, thanks to him, year in year out there will be a bank of purple foxgloves to brighten up the monotony of a train journey! I like the idea that some people will sleep through them and others will spot them out of the corner of their eye, some will enjoy a moment with them before they whizz by – either way, they will be there, lined up like passengers on a platform, waiting for their bee visitors.

LEFT After forest fires in the 1930s, planes were used to distribute seeds over inaccessible mountains in Honolulu.

ABOVE A railway full of beautiful poppy flowers.

Wet Balloon Bombs

Some people use balloons, like the old favourite water bombs of our childhood days. They explode on impact with the ground, but though they act as a suitable carrier for the seeds, they may not be particularly accurate and will leave the seeds vulnerable to attack by weather and seedeaters.

Place a funnel in the neck of the balloon and filter in the seeds and earth, then add water and fertilizer to the mix. The balloon bomb is good to go!

It needs to be made and launched within the same day so as to avoid rotting within the bomb.

Dry Balloon Bombs

Balloon bombs can be made without liquid and simply stuffed with seeds and earth and filled with helium; these are lots of fun to launch into the atmosphere – eventually they'll come down, though accuracy is highly variable.

Remember …

› It's important to use biodegradable balloons to prevent the remnants from polluting the environment. These can take 4–6 months to decompose, which might be a concern if they are floating about in the atmosphere, or if they fall but do not burst or are impenetrable. When will the seeds germinate?

› Be sure to choose your launch time carefully! Spring launching will still provide some rainfall – this will help land and degrade the balloon, as well as giving the seeds enough time to germinate when the right conditions occur. Autumn launching will give the balloon six months to land, degrade and germinate in time for spring.

Please note that it is a very variable and unpredictable method and at the end of the day Mother Nature will always decide.

Natural Seedbombs

The most environmentally sound way of making seedbombs is to use dirt.

Dirt, lovely dirt! Whether it's from your garden or a garden centre, it contains everything needed for a plant to grow into a healthy seedling.

Homemade compost, humus, green manure and tea and coffee waste, leaf

ABOVE LEFT Compost, manure or dirt: a natural choice for binding your seedbomb.

ABOVE Seedbombs can be any shape or size you choose – just bear in mind the launch.

OPPOSITE LEFT Cleverly designed seed grenades 'explode' on hitting the ground.

OPPOSITE RIGHT Innovative seedbomb bangles are a fashionable method of carrying your seeds.

mould and chicken manure can be used, as well as natural binding materials like waste paper pulp and clay.

The idea of a seedbomb is that it is aerodynamic and able to travel a distance when thrown, so it naturally tends to be ball-shaped. Seedbombs, seedballs, earth dumplings, clay bombs: they are generally always the same form – small, round and pocket- sized – but you can form them into any shape you like or put them into moulds. Obviously this may counterbalance the aerodynamics -– but you could simply lay them on the earth if you choose. Interesting 'ironic' design ideas include gun-shaped seedbombs that sprout to give the appearance of a green gun and fired terracotta pots in the shape of grenades that release an explosion of compost and seeds.

Or you can make heart shapes and even flower shapes – just make sure there is enough depth for the plant to grow.

Paper Bag Bombs

Fill brown paper bags with a mixture of compost and seeds, leaving enough room to twist the top of the bag and tie a knot in it. If the soil is moist, launch them on the same day. If the soil is bone dry, they may keep for a number of weeks in a cool, dry and dark place, but do check that they are not mouldy before you launch them.

Egg Bombs

Eggs can be blown and carefully filled with very dry powdery earth and seeds. They are quite fiddly to make but can be effective and are quite exciting when they smash onto the ground! You can decorate them or write messages as a tribute, or to mark a celebration.

Seedbomb Accessories

I've seen some pretty cool seed accessories such as little pots full of seeds that can be worn on a chain as a pendant, a key ring, a charm bracelet or as earrings, and bangle bombs made from transparent tubes that can be refilled time and again with seeds and sprinkled when and where you choose. As well as distributing seeds, these accessory vessels can be used to collect seeds on your travels. Whatever you use to make your seedbombs, think about the impact it will have on the environment, not just on the ground when it lands.

"A WEED IS NO MORE THAN A FLOWER IN DISGUISE."

James Russell Lowell

The Accidental Seedbomb

I have heard stories about people who have made their own seedbombs without realizing it. There is a world of anonymous dispersal happening without us even noticing and we wonder, 'How did that nigella end up in my garden? I know I didn't plant it...'

Tom' Bombs

You're having a picnic in the garden and a tomato falls on the ground. You pick it up and throw it in the flower bed without even thinking about it and a few weeks later notice a plant growing! Just let it do its thing and you'll have tomatoes just in time for the final summer barbecue. Delicious!

Boot Bombs

You can pick up seeds on your boots simply by walking around outdoors, in your own garden, at the local park, out in the fields, in the woods ... Your boots build up a fair bit of mud, which you knock off on the garden wall. The mud lands in the flower bed – and before you know it you have some guests in the garden.

Roadside Seedbombing

On outings, the tyre treads of your car pick up mud and dust; it spends most of its time parked in the driveway, next to a flower border. You pull up at some traffic lights and a clump of mud falls out of the tread. You drive off again, the wind blows the clump onto the verge, and when the next rain falls a tiny seed begins to germinate. Six weeks later you stop at those same traffic lights and think to yourself, 'How odd – aquilegias growing by the side of the road!'

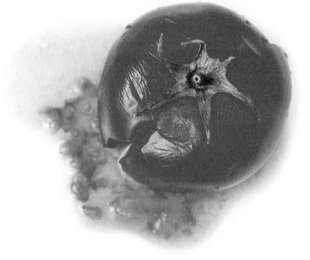

ABOVE A squashed tomato is the perfect accidental seedbomb.

Making Natural Seedbombs

There are many different recipes for making seedbombs and experimenting is part of the fun! Seedbombs are like miniature gardens – they will be the first soil the seedlings grow in and they need to supply nutrients and have good drainage, like a full-blown garden.

Some people make their own garden compost from household waste such as vegetable peelings and garden trimmings. Others buy it from the local garden centre, or dig earth out of their gardens.

Some seedbomb recipes are simply soggy compost and seeds compressed to make a ball, but these tend to break up in the air or on landing, leaving the seeds much more vulnerable.

It is best to use something to bind the seedbomb and make it hard enough to survive impact with the ground. Whatever you use needs to be water-soluble also, so that water can infiltrate the seedbomb, get to the seeds and break their dormancy.

I have seen some recipes where paper pulp made from egg boxes and office stationery waste has been mixed with compost. As the paper dries, it binds everything together.

Additions such as fertilizers, second-hand tea leaves and coffee grounds provide nutrients to boost the germination process and promote vigorous plant growth.

How much seed you use depends on the size of the seed; for example, the bigger the seed, the more compost and clay you'll need to add to the mixture and the bigger the bomb will need to be in order to accommodate them.

Be generous but not wasteful, because too many seeds will result in overcrowding and bad air circulation, which can make the plants suffer from fungal diseases such as stem rot.

The Seedbomb Base Recipe

Ingredients
Makes 6 sizeable seedsbombs

> 5 TABLESPOONS OF SEED COMPOST
> 4 TABLESPOONS OF TERRACOTTA CLAY POWDER
> 1 TEASPOON OF SEEDS (Note: Base this on poppy seeds as a size guide and add half a teaspoon more as the seeds go up in size)
> 1 TEASPOON OF CHILLI POWDER AS A PEST DETERRENT (optional)
> SPRINKLES OF WATER AT INTERVALS (the geek in me worked out it was about 20ml!)
> LIQUID FERTILIZER if NPK is absent in the compost

TIP To make larger quantities of seedbomb mixture, use the same proportions but measure using larger containers – mugs rather than tablespoons, for example – and use a bigger bowl, of course!

Remember when making seedbombs – the bigger the seed, the fewer seeds you need!

YOU WILL NEED

A bowl

A strong spoon

Kitchen towel or egg box

Water

A pen

Your hands and some elbow grease

An apron if yoou're worried about staining your clothes

And now for the Mixing and Making

1 Pour the compost into your bowl.
2 Pour the clay powder into your bowl.
3 Pour in the seeds.
4 Stir the dry ingredients together until well mixed.
5 Add water in small amounts at a time, mixing and adding until you form a dough-like consistency that sticks together nicely (not too sticky and not too dry).
6 Separate the mixture into six even lumps.
7 Roll each lump into a smooth ball.
8 Place the finished seedbombs on something absorbent like kitchen roll or an egg box.

See **SEEDBOMB Q&A** for any questions.

TIP When rolling your seedbombs, keep your palms flat to get a rounder shape. If your palms are slightly cupped, you get a shape not unlike a spinning top. Use your fingers to adjust the shape until you are happy with it.

What to do next

When you have made your seedbombs, you can:

1 Launch them immediately (if it is the right time of year); they will germinate quicker because they are still moist. Let them dry for a couple of hours so they are not too squidgy and don't lose their shape.
2 Dry them for up to 48 hours. The seeds will remain dormant until activated by water. They can be stored for up to two years and beyond, though some seeds may not germinate if left too long, especially vegetables.

TIP Dry your seedbombs on a sunny garden wall, shelf, windowsill, radiator or in the airing cupboard.

Seedbombs for Bees

The plants in this recipe are nectar-rich and a good food source for bees throughout the season. It is important that we grow plants that will provide a source of nectar for the bees, not only to help conserve their colonies but because they are major pollinators for wildflowers and food crops.

Some species of bee are facing extinction and over the last 70 years two species of bee have become nationally wiped out. The Bumblebee Conservation Trust (www. bumblebeeconservation.org) encourages small patches of wildflowers to be planted in field corners, gardens, waste ground, railways, roadside verges and motorway embankments. And that is where seedbombing is perfect for the job!

Plants

› FOXGLOVE *Digitalis purpurea*
› CLOVER *Trifolium pratense*
› WILD MARJORAM *Oreganum vulgare*
› CORNFLOWER *Centaurea cyanus*
› BETONY *Stachys officinalis*
› LESSER KNAPWEED *Centaurea nigra*

Seedbombs for Butterflies

Butterfly Conservation (www.butterfly-conservation. org) believes that butterflies and moths are a fundamental part of our heritage and are indicative of a healthy environment. It is important to grow food plants right through the season from when they come out of hibernation in spring to autumn, when they need to build up their energy reserves for winter. Grow plants that will provide hibernation,

somewhere to lay eggs, food for the larvae (caterpillars) and nectar for the butterfly.

Plants

- › FOXGLOVE *Digitalis purpurea*
- › RED CAMPION *Silene dioica*
- › OX-EYE DAISY *Leucanthemum vulgare*
- › LESSER KNAPWEED *Centaurea nigra*
- › FIELD SCABIOUS *Knautia arvensis*
- › CORN COCKLE *Agrostemma githago*

Seedbombs for Birds

The plants in this recipe attract insect larvae from which the birds will feed, as well as offering a rich seed source throughout the season. Birds help with seed dispersal and some seeds cannot germinate unless they have first passed through the digestive system of a bird.

The RSPB (www.rspb.org.uk) believes that a healthy bird population is indicative of a healthy planet and the human race depends on this.

Climate change, modern farming methods, road and rail networks, exploitation of our seas and expanding urban areas all pose an enormous threat to birds. We can try to increase the bird population by growing foodplants and creating healthy habitats for them to live and breed in.

Plants

- › SORREL *Rumex acetosa*
- › FIELD SCABIOUS *Knautia arvensis*
- › LESSER KNAPWEED *Centaurea nigra*
- › GREATER HAWKBUT *Leontodon autumnalis*
- › TEASEL *Dispascus fullonum*

ABOVE Some plants require a helping wing from birds before their seeds can germinate.

LEFT Bees are major pollinators for wildflowers and food crops.

Seedbombs for Senses

This recipe has been designed to fill your nostrils with a heavenly sweet scent, and attract and provide food for wildlife too. The plants have been chosen not only for their attractive scents, but for their colour and form.

Plants

› COWSLIP *Primula veris*
› FEVERFEW *Tanacetum parthenium*
› LADY'S BEDSTRAW *Gallium verum*
› WILD CHAMOMILE *Matricaria recutita*
› WILD MARJORAM *Origanum vulgare*
› MEADOWSWEET *Filipendula ulmaria*
› SWEET CICELY *Myrrhis odorata*

Healing seedbombs

These recipes have plants with healing properties for the mind, body and spirit. The plants will nourish and soothe, relax and enliven, as well as have culinary uses.

Well-being

› LEMON BALM *Melissa officinalis*
› BORAGE *Boragio officinalis*
› WILD MARJORAM *Oreganum vulgare*
› WILD CHAMOMILE *Matricaria recutita*
› LIQUORICE *Glycyrrhiza glabra*

Wake Up

› WILD MINT *Mentha arvensis*
› LEMON BALM *Melissa officinalis*
› LIQUORICE *Glycyrrhiza glabra*

Sleep Well

› ANISE *Pimpinella anisum*
› THYME *Thymus vulgaris*
› MUGWORT *Artemisia vulgaris*

Coughs, Colds and Headaches

› WILD CHAMOMILE *Matricaria recutita*
› LEMON BALM *Melissa officinalis*
› WILD MINT *Mentha arvensis*
› FEVERFEW *Tanacetum parthenium*
› COLTSFOOT *Tussilago farfara*
› ECHINACEA *Echinacea purpurea*
› FENNEL *Foeniculum vulgare*

ABOVE Certain plants such as wild marjoram promote relaxation and restfulness.

RIGHT Echinacea will flourish in a sunny spot.

Colourful seedbombs

The plants in this recipe are perfect for adding a splash of colour to the garden and also as a cut flower in the home. These recipes use plants that can be grown in sunny or shaded spots so you can have colour whatever the situation.

Plants for a Shady/Damp Spot

> SELF-HEAL *Prunella vulgaris*
> BEE BALM *Monarda didyma*
> BORAGE *Boragio officinalis*

Plants for a Sunny/Dry Spot

> COMMON POPPY *Papaver rhoeas*
> ARNICA *Arnica montana*
> ECHINACEA *Echinacea purpurea*

Foody plants

This section has recipes specifically for culinary uses, like roast dinners, soups and salads. The plants have medicinal uses too, for example to aid digestion or soothe common colds.

Allotment Seedbombs

> CHIVES *Allium schoenoprasum*
> SPINACH *Spinacia oleracea*
> BROAD BEAN *Vicia faba 'Sutton Dwarf'*
> COURGETTE *Cucurbita pepo*
> NASTURTIUM *Tropaeolum majus*

Wild Salad

> SORREL *Rumex acetosa edible*
> MARIGOLD *Calendua officinalis*
> BORAGE *Borago officinalis*
> SALAD BURNET *Sanguisorba minor*

Hot Salad

> NASTURTIUM *Tropaeolum majus*
> CHIVES *Allium schoenoprasum*
> MARIGOLD *Calendua officinalis*
> RADISH *Raphanus sativus*

What is Guerrilla Gardening?

Guerrilla gardening is seen as a relatively new movement but people have been gardening this way for centuries – it's just that no one put a name to it. Here are some historical key figures and events that 'sowed the seed' for this growing (and expanding!) movement.

Historical key points

The Diggers/True Levellers

In 1649, a time of great social unrest in England, a group called the 'True Levellers' was formed, led by Gerrard Winstanley. Later known as 'The Diggers', they were Protestant Christian agrarian radical communists who believed there is an ecological interrelationship between humans and nature and that the inherent links between people and their surroundings need to be recognized.

The Diggers took over vacant or common land in mid, south and south-east England and grew and distributed free food crops to their followers; but in 1651 the movement was crushed by the wannabe landowners inside Cromwell's Protectorate. People continue to be inspired by The Diggers and to celebrate through practice and events. Their belief that the land will provide if worked by a community force has transcended through time.

" *True freedom lies where a man receives his nourishment and preservation, and that is in the use of the earth.* "

Gerrard Winstanley

When the Phrase was Coined

The revolutionary city of New York – the 'Big Apple' – bore the fruit and sowed the seed of a group of people who have inspired the guerrilla gardeners of today. In 1973 the first community garden in New York was developed and was eventually given permission to be rented in 1974 as the Bowery Houston Community Farm and Garden. The group was called the 'Green Guerrillas' and some say that is where the 'Guerrilla Gardener' phrase was coined.

In 2002 the City of New York and the NYS Attorney General approved the garden in its entirety and ordered that its renovation be continued.

Johnny Appleseed Day March 11

This celebrates the work of American pioneer John Chapman (1774–1845), nicknamed 'Johnny Appleseed' because he used to collect apple seeds and spread them randomly everywhere he went. Orchards of over 15,000 trees sprung up all over Ohio, Illinois and Indiana due to this man! His work has made him a celebrated figure in America, through songs, comics and even a Disney animation, The Legend of Johnny Appleseed.

ABOVE Orchards of apple trees that provide a bounty of fresh delicious fruit.

LEFT Diggers farming in vacant land to grow and distribute free food crops to their followers.

Political Practice

'Guerrilla' is the Spanish word meaning a 'small army' that fights a stronger force. Perhaps the word 'seedbomb' has come about from its association with 'guerrilla', but if they are used responsibly they are certainly not belligerent bombs. Seedbombing is like a subdivision in a small army that could be called 'the stealth sowing division'!

It's important that guerrilla gardeners only choose areas that are clearly vacant, and plant non-invasive or native plants. A lot of guerrilla gardens are created on land that is to be developed with either housing or supermarkets. Unfortunately, impending constructions mean that some gardens have only a short life span. Fortunately, though, some gardens have successfully won over the community, landowners and the council and been granted tenancy.

The **POSITIVE** effects these 'pop up gardens' have on the community are priceless. New relationships are formed with people, with plants and with the environment. It only takes a handful of people to make a difference to an area; more hands make light work.

The **NEGATIVE** effects are that some people may not understand the ethos behind guerrilla gardening and instead see it as vandalism and crime. It may make some members of a community feel vulnerable, perhaps as if the neighbourhood is changing; they may worry that people/strangers are attracted to the garden and may be using it for antisocial behaviour. So it is important to communicate with the neighbourhood and keep the activities in the garden positive – this can easily be done through putting up posters and flyers and inviting people to join in with the gardening or event days.

A group of people wielding spades, forks and plants is bound to raise eyebrows and get people talking and naturally they'll want to join in.

Guerrilla gardens don't have to be full of plants that are just for ornamental purposes. The home-grown-food revolution is upon us and people are taking matters into their own hands to obtain certain levels of 'food security' by growing their own food locally and setting up community projects to educate people on how to grow their own food.

LEFT Guerrilla gardening can swiftly bring an urban environment closer to nature and enhance a sense of community.

LEFT Guerrilla gardening can promote respect for the global environment.

RIGHT Guerrilla gardeners feel that wasteland should be turned into somewhere productive and beautiful to be enjoyed by the community.

Groups and Individuals

Let's have a look at just a few examples of the many guerrilla gardening groups and individuals in the UK – but we'll start with New York's Green Guerrillas, because they were such an important catalyst to the movement and all research leads us back to them as being at its roots.

Green Guerrillas

This group was set up in New York in 1973 by an artist, Liz Christy, who assembled some of her friends and neighbours to clear out a vacant lot, where they created a vibrant community garden – the start of the New York guerrilla gardening movement.

The Green Guerrillas have beautified many desolate spots around the city and still operate today. Their mission is to bring the people together to create and educate through community gardens.

Glasgow Guerrilla Gardeners

" *Resistance is Fertile* "

In 2008 volunteers grouped together with the collective aim of beautifying Glasgow.

Organized events are publicized on their website (www.glasgowguerrillagardening. org.uk) and social network sites. Their projects include planting 10,000 bulbs, seedbombing dreary walkways and planting up wildflowers to attract bees in the city centre.

London Guerrilla Gardeners

In 2004 guerrillagardening.org was set up to document events that happened in London, network with likeminded people, dig in, seek advice and even get a troop number!

Brighton Guerrilla Gardeners

In May 2009 Brighton's first guerrilla garden was built by community troops. Wielding plants, forks and wheelbarrows, they transformed an abandoned petrol station from a bleak wasteland into the Lewes Road Community Garden. It was open for one blissful year before the 'heavies' came in and forced out all living things. What was once a place for family picnics, relaxing and bonding with people and plants has been claimed back by industry to become another block of consumer concrete.

The Human Shrub

One man (or woman) on a mission to make Colchester beautiful again!

In 2009 the human shrub took action against the council, who had drastically slashed their plants budget. Under the cover of moss and leaves he planted flowers and protested to the council, who reversed their plans to concrete over one in five roadside flower beds.

'THREE CHEERS FOR THE HUMAN SHRUB!'

Responsible Seedbombing

When you're launching seedbombs, there are lots of things to think about. Seedbombing responsibly includes identifying that the site you've chosen is right for the job, as well as making sure you get your aim straight – metaphorically as well as physically!

The Dos

Identify the site

> Is the site protected as a conservation area?Check this out by asking the council or researching on the internet or in your local library.
> Is the area privately owned? Make sure the land isn't used for agricultural purposes; you don't want to interfere with food crops.
> Is the site abandoned and will it benefit from being beautified? Ensure the site is not due for imminent construction and that the plants will thrive there.
> Choose your plants wisely – non-invasive, right plant, right place. Some plants are persistent, particularly invasive, and may suffocate and/or prevent the growth of other plants (especially precious native wildflowers). We don't want another bindweed or Himalayan balsam disaster on our hands!
> Use native plants. Using native plants maintains the natural balance of our wildlife, flora and fauna.
> Swot up on your nature knowledge. For hints and tips, see **NATURE KNOWLEDGE** (pages 94–95).
> Be wildlife aware. Encourage wildlife by using plants to attract bees, birds and butterflies.

Get Your Aim right

What is your aim? It's important to identify why you are choosing this method of gardening – it should essentially be for positive reasons. The ETHOS of seedbombing is that it's a fun and gentle form of dispersing seeds and beautifying desolate surroundings or domestic gardens.

- › **DO** foster orphaned land and fill urban voids with flowers.
- › **DO** grow food crops.
- › **DO** attract wildlife.
- › **DO** create a scenic route for both short local journeys and long motorway journeys.
- › **DO** unite a community through plants.
- › **DO** gain a sense of well-being

The Dont's

Identify the site

- › Don't throw seedbombs at people, or windows. Ensure that nothing or nobody will be damaged or harmed by your flying seedbombs.
- › Don't throw them into your neighbours' gardens without their consent. Save your seeds for something more positive than dealing with neighbourly disputes!
- › Don't throw them on land with inadequate growing conditions. If there is insufficient light and no obvious soil for the plants to anchor themselves into,

they will eventually perish.
- › Don't put yourself or anyone else in danger when launching your seedbombs. Although it is suggested that roadsides and railways are perfect for launching your seedbombs, don't go walking across busy roads and rail tracks – it's not worth putting yourself and others at risk of an accident.

Get Your Aim Wrong

Your aim is wrong if you are launching seedbombs to be antagonistic or are using them as a form of vandalism or coercion. It is also wrong if you have not given consideration to the plant and its new environment.

- › **DON'T** use seedbombs as a form of aggression or vandalism.
- › **DON'T** launch seedbombs that are not site-specific.
- › **DON'T** be reckless as it will have a negative impact on the community and the environment.

LEFT Be sure to research areas carefully before launching your seedbombs.

ABOVE Choose plants appropriate for the area, and which won't prevent other plant growth.

Nature Knowledge

By following a few simple maintenance procedures, you will give your plants the best chance of remaining healthy and vigorous and help to avoid attack from pests and diseases. You should act immediately upon any signs of pest damage or disease and take professional advice if necessary.

Deadheading
A flower's primary goal is to set seed. If you constantly cut off the dead heads the plant goes into overdrive, sending out more flowers in an effort to reproduce.

Pruning
Cutting back dead, damaged or diseased parts of the plant encourages growth and helps maintain vigour. Do this in spring or autumn and either compost the prunings or, if diseased, destroy them on a fire (use the ashes to condition the soil with potassium).

Division
To divide an overgrown plant, dig it up, remove as much of the soil from the roots as you can, and cut the plant in half with a sharp knife. Replant the parent plant in the original hole and the new plant in a new position. Water thoroughly before and after planting until established.

Root Cuttings
Take a healthy stout root, cut it into 5cm sections and pot it in well-drained compost with the tip of the cutting

just shy of the top of the soil. Do not overwater your cuttings. Shoots should emerge in early spring.

Air Circulation

Plants need good air circulation to help release waste gases and reduce the chances of disease and attack. Space plants according to size, which aids circulation and prevents competing for nutrients and soil water.

Food for Plants

There are 13 mineral nutrient elements that have a critical function in plant growth. There are two categories – micronutrients (needed in smaller quantities) and macronutrients (needed in higher doses and administered regularly by gardeners). Most of these nutrients are found in the soil but some need to be supplemented.

The Primary Macronutrients

NITROGEN (N) The plant utilizes nitrogen to produce leafy growth and for stem formation. Nitrogen requirements differ from plant to plant but as a rule the more leaf a plant produces (like cabbages or spinach), the higher its nitrogen need. Symptoms of deficiency are weak stems, stunted growth and yellowed or discoloured leaves. Peas make good companions for nitrogen-loving plants because they fix nitrogen in the soil.

PHOSPHORUS (P) Phosphorus plays a fundamental role in seed germination and root development, especially during its infancy. It is needed throughout a plant's life for healthy root growth, fruit and seed crops. Root vegetables such as carrots and parsnips benefit from generous doses of phosphorus. Symptoms of deficiency are low fruit yields, stunted growth and a purple tinge to the foliage.

POTASSIUM (K) is used in the process of building sugars and starches and is needed for vegetables and fruits. It encourages flower and fruit production and is a vital nutrient for maintaining health, vigour and resistance to disease. Potassium is found in wood ash and is perfect dug into the soil around your fruit trees and root vegetables. Symptoms of deficiency are scorched leaves, reduced fruit yields and low resistance to disease.

Micronutrients

› **IRON** Essential for the formation of chlorophyll.
› **COPPER** Aids reproductive growth and root metabolism.
› **MANGANESE/ZINC** Enzyme activation.
› **BORON** Aids sugar, carbohydrate, seed and fruit production.
› **MOLYBDENUM** Involved in the fixation of nitrogen.
› **CHLORIDE** Aids photosynthesis and plant metabolism.

Other Macronutrients

› **CALCIUM** A strengthening component of cell wall structure.
› **MAGNESIUM** Element of chlorophyll and vital for photosynthesis.
› **SULPHUR** Vital for plant vigour and resistance, root growth, seed production, vitamin development and chlorophyll formation.

LEFT Simple maintenance procedures will give your plants the best chance of remaining healthy and strong.

Chapter 5

WILDFLOWER DIRECTORY

A Bit of Soil Science

Soil is a combination of organic matter and rock in its final state of decomposition after millions of years of weathering. Soil is the primary carer for plants and its ability to provide effectively depends on the make-up of the soil. Additives can improve soil and growing conditions and help plants thrive.

When you come to read the plant directory you will see that for each entry there is a 'soil requirement'. This tells you that some plants are not fussy – that is, they'll grow happily in most moist, free-draining soils – while some thrive in a certain type of soil but fail to grow at all in another.

Structure and Texture

Have you ever heard other gardeners talking about having a 'sandy loam' or maybe a 'silty clay loam' and wondered, 'What on earth are they are talking about?' After all, soil is soil, isn't it?

Not so! Soil varies widely from area to area and there are a number of factors that affect how well a plant grows in it.

The pore spaces between the particles in the soil determine how well the soil absorbs water, air and nutrients and how long the soil retains them and leaches them out.

The ideal soil is 'loamy'; it is easy to work with and retains nutrients and water while allowing it to drain.

SANDY Larger pore spaces; leaches rapidly and dries out quickly.

CLAY Smaller spaces; holds on to water and is heavy.
LOAM A mixture of sand, clay and decaying organic materials.
SILT Rock particles that are coarser than clay and finer than sand.

Soil pH

Soil pH (potential of Hydrogen) is a measure on a scale of 0 to 14 of the soil's acidity or alkalinity.

pH is one of the most significant properties affecting nutrient availability for plants. Some plants prefer an acidic soil. These plants are called 'calcifuge' (lime-hating plants). Some plants prefer alkaline soils. These plants are called 'calcecoles' (lime-loving plants).

› 7 is neutral
› Alkaline is higher than pH 7
› Acidic is lower than pH 7
› 6.0 to 6.5 is the desirable range as it heightens microbial activity, allowing more nutrients to be released to the plants.
› Macronutrients are less obtainable in low pH soils.
› Micronutrients are less obtainable in high pH soils.

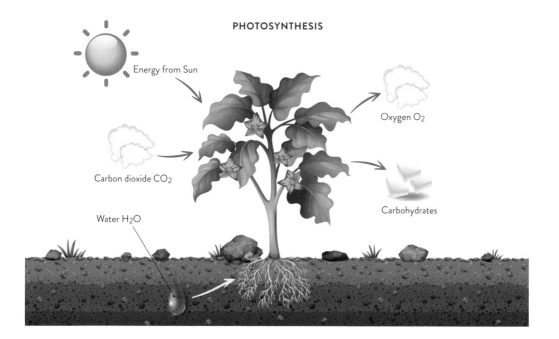

PHOTOSYNTHESIS

Energy from Sun

Oxygen O$_2$

Carbon dioxide CO$_2$

Carbohydrates

Water H$_2$O

A Bit of Botany

Some things going on within the plant are just too magical to understand. Here are some of the primary activities:

Photosynthesis

Plants are autotrophs – they can sustain life by making their own food.

Photosynthesis occurs primarily in the leaves; the chlorophyll in the chloroplasts captures radiant energy and generates carbohydrates and oxygen from carbon dioxide (CO_2) and water (H_2O).

CARBON DIOXIDE CO$_2$ is colourless, odourless and tasteless and is the main gas we exhale. Large amounts of CO_2 inhaled can be potentially lethal to humans and animals, which is why plants are so important – they use up the CO_2 in the atmosphere. When a plant dies and decomposes or is burned, CO_2 is released and returned to the atmosphere.

OXYGEN O$_2$ During photosynthesis, plants combine CO_2 and H_2O molecules to make carbohydrates. During this process some oxygen atoms are released.

WATER H$_2$0 acts as a solvent for minerals, allowing their absorption and transportation within the plant. Waterfilled cells keep the plant cells turgid. Plants deprived of water will wilt.

Transpiration

Water is evaporated through the leaves, a process called transpiration; it cools down the plant and opens the stomata (leaf pores used for gas exchange), which help with the intake of CO_2. Around 95% of the water taken up by the roots is transpired.

Osmosis

Plants take up soil water through the roots by 'osmosis', the movement of water molecules through a semipermeable membrane in the cell walls.

ABOVE Through photosynthesis, plants use sunlight, water and carbon dioxide to create oxygen and energy in the form of sugar.

And Now for the Plants

This directory is an introduction to 41 fantastic plants chosen to attract wildlife and for their scent, colour, medicinal and culinary properties, and suitability for seedbombing in the wild and at home. It is by no means an exhaustive list. We have picked a wide variety of plants, from the robust teasel to the delicate poppy.

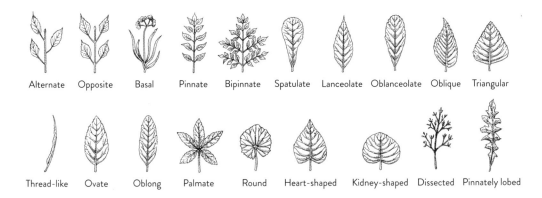

Alternate · Opposite · Basal · Pinnate · Bipinnate · Spatulate · Lanceolate · Oblanceolate · Oblique · Triangular

Thread-like · Ovate · Oblong · Palmate · Round · Heart-shaped · Kidney-shaped · Dissected · Pinnately lobed

Leaf out of this Book

Leaves are elegantly crafted into many different shapes and sizes with the primary goal of harvesting light. They must be sheetlike, thin and translucent (to allow light to reach the innermost cells). They must have stalks, which may develop in an opposite or alternate pattern on the stem and elevate the leaves to positions where they can track the movement of the sun throughout the day.

There is an unlimited diversity in leaf characteristics. Some come in single blades or are divided into leaflets; some have leaf margins, which can be whole, toothed or wavy. All these characteristics are what botanists use to identify and describe a plant. Below are just some examples of leaf shapes referred to in this directory.

"TO FORGET HOW TO DIG THE
EARTH AND TO TEND THE SOIL
IS TO FORGET OURSELVES."

Mahatma Gandhi

Wild Chamomile

Matricaria chamomilla

Chamomile was cultivated as early as the Neolithic period and has been used for centuries as a 'cure-all' medicinal plant. A great companion plant as its strong, aromatic flowers attract beneficial insects that feed on pest predators, such as aphids.

FAMILY
Asteraceae/Compositae

NATIVE TO
Southern Europe

HEIGHT/SPREAD
60 x 40cm

HABITAT
Roadsides, railways, waste ground, fields, arable land

THRIVES IN
Full sun/partial shade

SOIL
Most soil types; tolerates poor soils

LIFESPAN
Annual

FLOWERS
May–August

FORM
Upright

LEAF FORM
Upper: Bipinnate; Lower: Tripinnate

POLLINATED BY
Insects

NOTE
Few allergic reactions to chamomile have been reported

CONSERVATION STATUS
No known conservation issues

STEMS Branched, upright, smooth stem.
LEAVES The long and narrow alternate leaves can be harvested fresh from the plant for medicinal uses.
FLOWERS Yellow and comb-like centres) and surrounded by 10–20 white petals. Harvest the flowers for medicinal uses when open and fresh or dry for later use. It takes 20–35 days from flower to seed.
SEEDS 1mm elongated, light brown and ridged.
LAUNCH SEEDBOMBS April–May and August–September.
GERMINATION TIME 1–2 weeks.
HARVESTING SEEDS Seeds ripen July to September.

PLANT CARE Don't cut back the foliage before flowering as the flower production will reduce dramatically. To remove aphids wash off with a strong jet of water.
PESTS AND DISEASES Can suffer aphid attacks which attract hungry ladybirds. Generally disease-free but susceptible to rust, downy mildew and powdery mildew.
CULINARY AND MEDICINAL USES Chamomile has soothing properties and is used to help alleviate conditions such as nervousness, anxiety, hysteria, headaches, stomach pains, indigestion, colds and flu. Also used as a poultice for swellings, sprains and bruises. Steep for 15 minutes then drink for a gentle sleep aid.

Common Poppy

Papaver rhoeas

The poppy is one of the most commonly recognized wildflowers. During World War I, common poppies bloomed in waste grounds and served as a vivid reminder of the battles that took place; they are now an iconic flower to military veterans as the symbol of remembrance.

FAMILY
Papaveraceae

NATIVE TO
Europe

HEIGHT/SPREAD
60 x 20cm

HABITAT
Roadsides, railways, waste ground, fields, cultivated beds

THRIVES IN
Full sun

SOIL
Grows on most moist free-draining soils (can suffer on heavy clay)

LIFESPAN
Annual

FLOWERS
June–August

FORM
Wiry, clump-forming

LEAF FORM
Pinnately divided

POLLINATED BY
Beetles, bees, flies

NOTE
The latex in the seed pods is a mild narcotic and slightly sedative. The seeds are NOT toxic to humans.

CONSERVATION STATUS
No known conservation issues

STEMS The stems grow from a big taproot and are upright, wiry and branching; they are green with a purplish tinge and have tough hairs.

LEAVES Alternate divided, serrated pairs of narrow, toothed leaves.

FLOWERS Hermaphrodite, four to six vivid red, wrinkled petals with a black blotch at the base. Yellow and brown anthers radiate from the central ovary; the ovary ripens and sheds seeds 3–4 weeks after flowering.

SEEDS The seed pod is small, green-blue and shaped like a pepperpot – as it dries and browns, the holes open around the top edge, and as the wind blows the seeds are released from the holes. They are tiny round black dots. The average number of seeds per seed pod is 1,360. The number of seeds per plant ranges from 10,000 to 60,000. The seeds can remain viable in the soil for up to 8 years.

LAUNCH SEEDBOMBS March–April and September–October.

GERMINATION TIME 1–6 weeks.

HARVESTING SEEDS Seeds ripen for harvesting between August and September.

PLANT CARE Poppy self-seeds readily and may need deadheading to prevent prolific spread (use this procedure as part of your seed-harvesting routine). As long as they have sunshine they are happy. Poppies thrive best in disturbed land; give your seeds a helping hand at germinating by annually digging over the spot where they have fallen.

PESTS AND DISEASES Can suffer attacks from greedy aphids and be susceptible to downy mildew.

CULINARY AND MEDICINAL USES Ancient Egyptians pressed the seed to obtain cooking oil, which was used with honey to create a sweet confection. The seeds have a nutty flavour and are sometimes used for baking. Common poppy has been used as a mild pain reliever and a sedative and to treat coughs, sleeplessness and digestive problems. Common poppy is not addictive, but the seed pods do contain alkaloids and should only be used under the supervision of a qualified herbalist.

OTHER USES Dried petals can be added to potpourri.

Corn Cockle

Agrostemma githago

Corn cockle is easy to grow in any position and ideal for naturalizing in a wildflower meadow. It is a quick grower and produces slender stems carrying mauve flowers, which attract birds, bees and butterflies (the flowers close at night). The whole plant is delicately covered with fine silver hairs.

FAMILY
Caryophyllaceae

NATIVE TO
Europe

HEIGHT/SPREAD
120 x 30cm

HABITAT
Roadsides, railways, waste ground, fields

THRIVES IN
Full sun/partial shade

SOIL
Tolerates most moist soils

LIFESPAN
Hardy annual

FLOWERS
June–August

FORM
Upright, slender

LEAF FORM
Lanceolate

POLLINATED BY
Long-tongued insects like butterflies, moths and bees

NOTE
All parts of the plant are poisonous if ingested

CONSERVATION STATUS
Intensive mechanized farming has put the plant at risk and it is now virtually extinct in the wild

STEMS Fuzzy, branched, slender stems.

LEAVES The stem is lined with opposite hairy, narrow lanceolate, grey-green leaves.

FLOWERS Delicate five-petalled pink scentless flowers. Each petal bears two or three irregular black lines. There are five narrowly pointed green sepals; these exceed the petals and are joined at the bottom to form a downy furrowed tube, which develops into a seed capsule.

SEEDS Many seeds are produced in the capsule – quite possibly the coolest seed I've ever seen!

LAUNCH SEEDBOMBS May and September.

GERMINATION TIME 1 week.

HARVESTING SEEDS Collecting the seed early in the season avoids seed-borne disease.

PLANT CARE This upright fast-growing plant needs support with stakes to avoid wind damage. Deadhead to prolong flowering and encourage more flower buds. Needs regular irrigation but suffers if waterlogged. Fertilize with NPK when the plant is juvenile.

PESTS AND DISEASES Generally pest- and disease-free.

CULINARY AND MEDICINAL USES Not recommended for consumption.

Red Campion

Silene dioica

Red campion is a relatively short-lived perennial. The male and female flowers are borne on separate plants. Often associated with woodlands and country roadside verges but can be grown in cultivated beds. It has a long flowering period right through to autumn.

FAMILY
Caryophyllaceae

NATIVE TO
Europe

HEIGHT/SPREAD
90 x 30cm

HABITAT
Roadsides, railways, waste ground, fields, maritime, cliffs and seabird crevices

THRIVES IN
Full sun/partial shade

SOIL
Drought tolerant; grows on most soils but thrives on free-draining, moist, calcareous soils

LIFESPAN
Herbaceous perennial

FLOWERS
May–October

FORM
Clump-forming

LEAF FORM
Ovate

POLLINATED BY
Bees, flies

NOTE
No known hazards

CONSERVATION STATUS
No known conservation issues

STEMS Wiry, strong, upright branched, round downy stems.

LEAVES Deep green in opposite paired, slightly sticky leaves.

FLOWERS Downy, somewhat sticky branching stems hold dioecious unscented rose pink flowers, which consist of five deeply notched petals joined at the base to form an urn shape and surrounded by a purple/brown calyx.

SEEDS The seed pod is an ovoid capsule containing numerous seeds. When dry, the seed pod opens at the apex as several teeth curve back to release the seeds. These are kidney-shaped, 3mm long, and the colour varies from red/brown to black.

Microscopically, they have a wonderful bobbly texture.

LAUNCH SEEDBOMBS Any time of year.

GERMINATION TIME 1–2 weeks.

HARVESTING SEEDS Seed ripens July onwards. The female plant produces thousands of seeds per season, which can remain viable for many years.

PLANT CARE Red campion is a low-maintenance plant and may only need autumn dividing if it has become too big.

PESTS AND DISEASES Relatively pest- and disease-free. Suffers with prolonged periods of waterlogging.

CULINARY AND MEDICINAL USES No known culinary or medicinal uses.

Betony

Stachys officinalis

Supposedly taken from the Celtic word *bewton*, meaning 'good for the head', Betony is said to have been one of the most important medicinal plants for Anglo Saxons. Betony is a slow-growing, long-lived hardy perennial found in dry grassland, meadows, open woods and slopes.

STEMS Like all plants in the *Lamiaceae* family, *Stachys officinalis* has distinctive square purplish stems with a branching leaf axis.

LEAVES Pairs of alternate, stalkless, narrow, ovate, fluffy leaves are borne sparsely towards the top of the stem. Most of the foliage is formed at the base of the stem and the leaves are larger, heart-shaped and rough to the touch with fine, short, fluffy hairs and toothed margins. The entire surface of the leaf has glands containing bitter, aromatic oil.

FLOWERS Short flower spikes grow on the top of the stem; further groups of flowers grow at intervals up the stem, a characteristic of betony. The rich purplish-pink hermaphrodite flowers are tubular and two-lipped; the upper lip forms a hood and the lower lip has two short side lobes and a large wide middle lobe.

SEEDS The seeds are 0.3mm long and rusty-brown coloured, with an angular shape.

LAUNCH SEEDBOMBS March–September or October–February because the seeds need a period of chill to break their dormancy and speed up germination.

GERMINATION TIME Irregular – often takes between 30 and 90 days.

HARVESTING SEEDS Seeds ripen from July to October. Cut the stems several inches above the soil line and strip the leaves off.

PLANT CARE Betony is frost-hardy and drought tolerant. Ensure good air circulation and drainage, and occasionally weed around the plant to allow it to spread. Divide mature clumps in the spring or autumn to increase health and vigour and make more plants.

PESTS AND DISEASES Young growth can be attacked by slugs. Seldom attacked by diseases but can suffer from root rot caused by a fungus present in boggy conditions.

CULINARY AND MEDICINAL USES The leaves and flowering tops make a good caffeine-free substitute for tea. Brewed in water to taste, it has all the good qualities of normal tea and bypasses the bad ones. Modern herbalists may prescribe Betony to help treat conditions such as high blood pressure, anxiety, heartburn, migraine and stress headaches, and as an antiperspirant.

FAMILY
Lamiaceae/Labiatae

NATIVE TO
Europe, western Asia and North Africa

HEIGHT/SPREAD
70 x 45cm

HABITAT
Roadsides, railways, waste ground, woodlands, grassy clifftops, grassy banks

THRIVES IN
Full sun/dappled shade

SOIL
Tolerates poor soils and thrives on damp soils

LIFESPAN
Hardy perennial

FLOWERS
July–September

FORM
Hardy perennial

LEAF FORM
Upper: Lanceolate; Lower: oblong/heart-shaped

POLLINATED BY
Bees

NOTE
Not recommended during pregnancy

CONSERVATION STATUS
Rare in Northern Scotland and the Republic of Ireland, where it is classified as Endangered and protected by the 1999 Flora Protection Order.

Cornflower

Centaurea cyanus

Cornflower was once a common weed of cornfields and arable land, but due to modern intensive farming practices and the use of herbicides, its presence has been drastically cut. With their attractive flower heads, they are much sought-after for gardens and flower arrangements.

FAMILY
Compositae/Asteraceae

NATIVE TO
Europe

HEIGHT/SPREAD
90 x 30cm

HABITAT
Roadsides, railways,
waste ground, fields

THRIVES IN
Full sun (suffers in shade)

SOIL
Thrives on most soils;
tolerates poor soils
(suffers in drought)

LIFESPAN
Hardy annual

FLOWERS
June–August

FORM
Slender

LEAF FORM
Lanceolate

POLLINATED BY
Long-tongued insects
like butterflies,
moths and bees

NOTE
Poisonous to cats if
ingested

CONSERVATION STATUS
In 1990, Cornflower
sightings dramatically
declined in the UK.
Various charities
are working towards
preventing extinction.

STEMS The flowers appear at the top of downy grey-green slender hollow stems on plump, hard involucres with bracts resembling overlapping tiles with black jagged edges.

LEAVES Lanceolate alternate, stalkless, downy grey-green leaves.

FLOWERS Cornflower has a compound head of ruffled, vivid-blue tubular flowers; on the outer edge sit the large blue flowers and in the middle of the flower head rest the smaller, brilliant- purple flowers.

SEEDS The seed head opens as it dries to reveal many seeds surrounded by soft silver fluff, which aids wind dispersal. The seeds are 5mm long and have a pearly white, shiny colour with a tuft of light-brown bristles.

LAUNCH SEEDBOMBS March–May but autumn launching produces larger, earlier-flowering plants.

GERMINATION TIME 1–2 weeks

HARVESTING SEEDS Harvest cornflower seeds throughout summer as the flower dies; it can be incorporated as part of the deadheading routine.

PLANT CARE The wiry plants may need some support to prevent them from collapsing or from disorderly growth. Deadheading helps to extend the flowering season. Cut the faded flower heads down to the ground in autumn, and compost the spent brown stems. Can be invasive so cut seed heads off before self-seeding and occasionally divide and thin out the plant.

PESTS AND DISEASES Cornflowers are relatively pest-free apart from one bothersome pest – the aphid! Cornflowers can suffer from rust and from powdery mildew.

CULINARY AND MEDICINAL USES
The blue dye obtained from the petals is edible and used for colouring sweets. The young shoots and flowers can be used in salads and as a garnish. Cornflower is rarely used in modern medicine. A tonic can be made and used as a mild purgative or as a mouthwash. Externally it can be used as an anti-inflammatory and astringent herb for skin cleansing and the infused blossoms can be made into an eyewash.

OTHER USES A blue dye is obtained from the petals. Mixed with alum-water it dyes linen and wool and is also added to cosmetic products like shampoo and dyes.

Lesser Knapweed

Centaurea nigra

Considered a weed in Australia and the USA, this wildflower is common in Europe. It grows in large colonies and is a vital source of food for birds, bees, butterflies and moths as it is nectar-rich and provides autumn and winter seeds for many birds.

STEMS Tough, wiry, prostrate, woody, roughly hairy and grooved stems.

LEAVES The leaf shape throughout the plant varies; the upper leaves are dull green, stalkless, downy and lanceolate. The lower leaves are stalked and deeply lobed, some with coarse teeth, and are often confused with the thistle.

FLOWERS Lesser knapweed flowers are hermaphrodite and are purple, thistle-like and come in two forms, rayed and un-rayed. The flower sits on a hard head of overlapping bracts.

SEEDS As the hard seed head dries, it opens to release around 60 seeds to be dispersed by the wind; they can travel many miles. The seeds are 5mm long, pearly white with lengthwise stripes, little notches at the base and a tuft of short light-brown bristles at the top.

LAUNCH SEEDBOMBS Early spring through to autumn, but this is such a brilliant plant and if conditions are suitable it will germinate and grow at any time of the year.

GERMINATION TIME 1–2 weeks.

HARVESTING SEEDS Seeds ripen for harvesting from August–October. Collect when plump and hard and all the petals are absent.

PLANT CARE Leaving the seed heads uncut after flowering provides food for garden birds, but there will also be a risk of unwanted spread of the plant through self-seeding. Lesser knapweed is an easy plant to grow and once established can tolerate considerable amounts of neglect. It can be invasive as it will self-seed freely, so cut seed heads off early. Divide the plant in autumn once every three years to maintain its health and vigour. The plant will suffer in damp and in acid soils.

PESTS AND DISEASES Knapweed is a tough cookie and relatively pest-free, the only threat being birds eating the seeds, but there are more than enough seeds to go around! Seldom attacked by any diseases.

CULINARY AND MEDICINAL USES
The petals can be eaten raw, sprinkled over salads or used as a garnish. Historically used as a diuretic and tonic; made into an ointment, it was used externally to help heal wounds and skin ailments such as cuts and bruises. It was also used to assist with sore throats and bleeding gums.

FAMILY
Asteraceae

NATIVE TO
Europe and introduced into the US and Australia

HEIGHT/SPREAD
65 x 30cm

HABITAT
Roadsides, railways, waste ground, cliffs, grassland

THRIVES IN
Sun and semi-shade; tolerant of maritime conditions

SOIL
Drought-resistant; thrives in most soil types; requires well-drained soil; tolerates poor soil

LIFESPAN
Hardy herbaceous perennial

FLOWERS
June–September

FORM
Clumps of upright stems

LEAF FORM
Upper: Lanceolate;
Lower: Lobed

POLLINATED BY
Long-tongued insects like butterflies, moths and bees

NOTE
No known hazards

CONSERVATION STATUS
Rare in some parts of Scotland

Field Scabious

Knautia arvensis

A tap-rooted herbaceous perennial that soars above its neighbouring plants. The lower leaves are thistle-like, while the upper are lance-shaped. It receives regular visits from bees, butterflies, moths, hoverflies and birds.

FAMILY
Dipsacaceae

NATIVE TO
Europe and Asia

HEIGHT/SPREAD
10 x 30cm

HABITAT
Roadsides, railways, waste ground, fields

THRIVES IN
Full sun
(suffers in deep shade)

SOIL
Drought tolerant; grows on most soils but thrives on free-draining calcareous soils

LIFESPAN
Hardy perennial herb

FLOWERS
July–October

FORM
Upright, clump-forming

LEAF FORM
Upper: Pinnately lobed;
Lower: Lanceolate

POLLINATED BY
Long-tongued insects like butterflies, moths and bees

NOTE
No known hazards

CONSERVATION STATUS
No known conservation issues

STEMS Round stems, branched and coarsely covered in whitish hairs.

LEAVES Dull green leaves form a basal rosette.

FLOWERS Delicate, rounded flat flower heads are usually in shades of purple or mauve and comprise around 50 tiny, densely packed, four-lobed flowers with protruding pink anthers (hence its likeness to a pin cushion).

SEEDS The seeds are achenes, and are light brown, cylindrical, slightly hairy and 5mm long. They fall to the ground when they are ripe.

LAUNCH SEEDBOMBS March and September.

GERMINATION TIME Erratic, up to 30 days.

HARVESTING SEEDS August–October.

PLANT CARE Field scabious is an invasive species and may need controlling if grown in a cultivated bed – thin out by digging up in the autumn and destroying. The plant overwinters as a rosette of dark green leaves. Cut off spent flower heads and compost them.

PESTS AND DISEASES Can be attacked by aphids. Generally disease-free.

CULINARY AND MEDICINAL USES
No known culinary uses. Historically has been used as a medicinal herb to help treat skin disorders, cuts, burns, bruises and boils, and also for blood purification.

Wild Teasel

Dipsacus fullonum

A biennial plant, teasel forms a prickly rosette of leaves in the first year of growth and the flowering stem emerges in the following growing season. Common names include prickly beehives and church brooms.

FAMILY
Dipsacaceae

NATIVE TO
Europe, North Africa, Asia

HEIGHT/SPREAD
200 x 80cm

HABITAT
Roadsides, railways, waste ground, fields, riverbanks

THRIVES IN
Full sun/partial shade

SOIL
Most free-draining soils

LIFESPAN
Bienniel

FLOWERS
July–August

FORM
Upright, clump-forming

LEAF FORM
Basal: Ovate;
Upper: Lanceolate

POLLINATED BY
Bees

NOTE
No known hazards

CONSERVATION STATUS
No known conservation issues

STEMS Stout upright stems are produced during the second year of growth. Downward prickles grow in ridges along the stem.

LEAVES The first season of growth produces a basal rosette of pale green prickly leaves. The leaves on the flowering stem form a kind of bowl-shape, which collects water.

FLOWERS The spiny cone-like flower heads are 3–10cm long and are covered in tiny hermaphrodite purplish tubular flowers, 10–15cm long, occurring in a ring around the head. The base of the flower head has several leaf-like bracts curving upward.

SEEDS There are approximately 2,000 flowers per flower head; each one produces a 4–5mm long, sandy-brown furrowed seed.

LAUNCH SEEDBOMBS February–May and August–October.

GERMINATION TIME 1–4 weeks.

HARVESTING SEEDS August–October.

PLANT CARE Because they seed freely they can grow in unwanted places; to prevent this, pull out unwanted seedlings. As the plants die down they leave a large area of bare ground ready for the seeds to germinate into new plants. Will withstand harsh weather conditions.

PESTS AND DISEASES Aphids. Generally disease-free.

CULINARY AND MEDICINAL USES No known edible uses. Used to help treat fractures as it contains nutrients that strengthen bones, cartilage and sinews. May also help stomach complaints, and promote blood circulation and energy.

Greater Hawkbit

Leontodon autumnalis

Considered a weed, this wildflower is in the same family as dandelion. It has a long flowering season, provides late-season colour and nectar for a variety of insects, and is a foodplant for birds. It's extremely hardy, and able to grow on sites with regular disturbance such as cut and grazed fields.

FAMILY
Asteraceae/Compositae

NATIVE TO
Europe

HEIGHT/SPREAD
30 x 30cm

HABITAT
Roadsides, railways, waste ground, fields, shores

THRIVES IN
Full sun

SOIL
Drought tolerant; grows on most soils

LIFESPAN
Hardy perennial herb

FLOWERS
June–October

FORM
Sprawling/low

LEAF FORM
Lanceolate

POLLINATED BY
Long-tongued insects like butterflies, moths and bees

NOTE
Prolonged ingestion of the herb could cause side effects

CONSERVATION STATUS
No known conservation issues

STEMS The stems are thin, tough, branched and round.

LEAVES A low-growing basal rosette of long, deeply cut narrow leaves.

FLOWERS Yellow 'composite' flat flower with square-tipped petals with a serrated edge and a reddish-tinged underside. A slightly hairy involucre rests directly below the petals; it is pale green with yellow reddish tinges.

SEEDS The seeds are cylindrical, smooth, light brown, with a feather-like pappus of branching hairs.

LAUNCH SEEDBOMBS Any time of year.

GERMINATION TIME 1–3 weeks.

HARVESTING SEEDS Once pollinated, the petals close and the fruit forms. Cut off the seed head before it opens to release the seeds.

PLANT CARE A hardy plant that needs little attention. Greater hawkbit relies upon seed for regeneration so any unwanted repopulation of the plant can be managed by clipping the flowers off before they seed.

PESTS AND DISEASES Generally pest- and disease-free.

CULINARY AND MEDICINAL USES Fresh leaves can be added to salads and the roasted root made into tea and a coffee substitute. For many centuries the plant has been used as a diuretic, to detoxify and to assist in improving bone health.

Mugwort

Artemisia vulgaris

Regarded as a roadside weed, this rhizomous aromatic perennial was known in ancient times as one of the most powerful medicinal herbs. A valuable foodplant for Lepidoptera, which feed on the leaves and flowers.

FAMILY
Asteraceae/Compositae

NATIVE TO
Europe, Asia, North
Africa, North America

HEIGHT/SPREAD
200 x 70cm

HABITAT
Roadsides, railways, waste
ground, fields

THRIVES IN
Full sun/partial shade

SOIL
Drought tolerant; grows
on most soils but thrives
on nitrogen-rich moist
soils

LIFESPAN
Herbaceous perennial
herb

FLOWERS
July–September

FORM
Bushy, dense, spreading

LEAF FORM
Pinnatipartite to
Bipinnate

POLLINATED BY
Wind

NOTE
Not recommended
during pregnancy or
while breast-feeding.
Prolonged ingestion could
cause side effects

CONSERVATION STATUS
No known
conservation issues

STEMS The upright stem has a red-purplish tinge.

LEAVES The dark green, deeply indented, pinnate, feather-like leaves have a downy white underside.

FLOWERS Panicles of 5mm-long reddish-yellow hermaphrodite flowers.

SEEDS Each stem produces up to 9,000 glabrous seeds.

LAUNCH SEEDBOMBS February–March.

GERMINATION TIME 1–2 weeks.

HARVESTING SEEDS August–October.

PLANT CARE Mugwort is vigorous and doesn't require any special attention. Deadhead before it sets seed. Note: It has growth inhibitors in its roots that may reduce vigour of neighbouring plants.

PESTS AND DISEASES Generally pest-free but can suffer from powdery mildew.

CULINARY AND MEDICINAL USES All of it can be used fresh or dried. Its leaves have a mild sage aroma and have been used to flavour beer and meat and fish dishes. Young leaves can be boiled as a pot herb or used in salad. Pick the leaves and buds shortly before it flowers. Historically used as an anti-inflammatory and antiseptic, and to help alleviate digestive issues, coughs and colds, fevers and gynaecological problems.

Meadowsweet

Filipendula ulmaria

Meadowsweet has been used as a medicinal plant since ancient times. It was a very sacred herb to the Druids for its medicinal properties, and the Anglo Saxons used it to flavour a drink made from fermented honey called medu, which means 'mead' – hence its common name of meadowsweet.

STEMS The stems are tall, upright/arching, reddish-purple, angular and furrowed; it branches nearer the top and bears long petioled alternate leaves.

LEAVES Fern-like, deeply veined leaves comprising two to five pairs of ovate, serrated, dark green, almond-scented leaflets with downy undersides. There are three to five terminal leaflets at the end of each leaf.

FLOWERS The flowers are sweetly scented, hermaphrodite and composed of panicled cymes of creamy-white flower clusters; each flower has five petals and over 20 protruding stamens, giving the flowers a delicate fuzzy appearance.

SEEDS The seeds are 1mm long, tan-coloured (when dry) and are formed in globe-like green clusters of six to ten seeds. The seeds can be dispersed via water and can float for several weeks before bedding in the riverbank.

LAUNCH SEEDBOMBS March–September.

GERMINATION TIME Up to 4 weeks.

HARVESTING SEEDS The seeds ripen from August to September and can be sown green.

PLANT CARE Meadowsweet has a tendency to self-seed everywhere; to control this, remove the faded flowers before the seeds form. Divide in spring or autumn. Meadowsweet likes to be watered copiously and regularly. The plant is deciduous and dies down in the winter; after the birds have fed from the seeds, cut back in (autumn) to prevent frost damage.

PESTS AND DISEASES Generally pest-free. Can suffer from powdery mildew and rust fungus.

CULINARY AND MEDICINAL USES Meadowsweet flowers have been used to flavour beverages and made into syrup for fruit salad. The leaves flavour soups and stews. Meadowsweet is thought to relieve pain and can be used as an anti-inflammatory and to treat digestive and diuretic problems, heartburn, headaches, menstrual cramps, common colds, sickness and rheumatic pain. A decoction can be made to use externally as a wash for wounds and to soothe sore eyes.

OTHER USES A black dye can be obtained from the roots and a yellow dye from the plant tops. The flower buds provide an essential oil.

FAMILY
Rosaceae

NATIVE TO
Europe and Asia

HEIGHT/SPREAD
120 x 45cm

HABITAT
Roadside ditches, riverside, woodland, meadows, wild gardens, cultivated beds

THRIVES IN
Full sun/partial shade

SOIL
Most moist, well-drained soils

LIFESPAN
Hardy herbaceous perennial herb

FLOWERS
June–August

FORM
Clump-forming, upright

LEAF FORM
Irregularly pinnate/ovate

POLLINATED BY
Bees, beetles, flies

NOTE
Not to be ingested if you are allergic to aspirin, and not recommended during pregnancy or for nursing mothers or children under 12 years

CONSERVATION STATUS
No known conservation issues

Cowslip

Primula veris

Cowslips are a well-loved English countryside wildflower. Their populations declined in the last century, but having been recorded as a protected species, and due to changes in agricultural practice, they are staging a revival. They are increasingly appearing on motorways and roadsides.

STEMS Cowslips grow in clumps very close to the ground. The first emerging leaves are tight coils, which unroll to form a rosette from which emerge stocky, round, pale green, single-flowering stems. The cowslip's stem is stout, light pale green, fuzzy/downy, upright and round.

LEAVES The leaves are oval, fresh green, crinkly, toothed and tough, covered with downy hairs and around 15cm long and 6cm wide, with paler green to white midribs and veins.

FLOWERS Hermaphrodite clusters (umbel) of 10–30 funnel-shaped, orange-based, deep-yellow nodding flowers, 9–15mm long, with five heart-shaped petals that usually droop to one side of the stem and are sweetly fragrant. The flowers are followed by clustered seed pods.

SEEDS The seed pod is an ovoid capsule containing several brown/black seeds, which take a while to ripen and dry; eventually in July they open at the apex, where several teeth curve back to release the seeds.

LAUNCH SEEDBOMBS July – If collected and sown while still green, it will not go dormant and will germinate rapidly

September – Will be dormant already and need the cold winter months to break dormancy.

GERMINATION TIME 6 months (the following spring).

HARVESTING SEEDS Seed pods ripen from July to August and can be sown green or dried for later use.

PLANT CARE If grown in a lawn, don't mow around the plants until they have finished flowering. Cowslip will self-seed on the lawn; the seedlings can be pricked out and grown on in pots. Suffers if waterlogged. Divide from September after flowering. Cut off and compost any browning or yellowed leaves.

PESTS AND DISEASES Caterpillars may be found around and underneath the leaf rosette in springtime. Aphids may attack the soft tissue of the plant. Mosaic virus, crown rot, downy mildew and leaf spot.

CULINARY AND MEDICINAL USES The leaves have been used in salads and to make wine and vinegar. Dried leaves can be made into a tea, and the flowers into a jam conserve. Cowslips are thought to help alleviate rheumatic pains, spasms and cramps.

FAMILY
Primulaceae

NATIVE TO
Europe

HEIGHT/SPREAD
25 x 25cm

HABITAT
Roadsides, motorway banks, railways, waste ground, fields, meadows, maritime, woodland, lawns

THRIVES IN
Full sun/partial shade

SOIL
Most moist, nutrient-rich, free-draining soils

LIFESPAN
Hardy herbaceous perennial

FLOWERS
April–May

FORM
Low-growing clumps

LEAF FORM
Ovate

POLLINATED BY
Long-tongued insects like butterflies, moths and bees

NOTE
Not recommended during pregnancy

CONSERVATION STATUS
Absent in northerly areas including much of north-west Scotland. Should not be collected in the wild.

Red Clover

Trifolium pratense

Red clover is a wild plant with a sprawling habit, usually found in fields and meadows and unattended wasteland. It is used as grazing fodder for livestock for its high protein content and high yields. It also has a number of medicinal benefits for ailments.

STEMS Its rhizomatous roots send out runners, which produce numerous sprawling, herbaceous, slightly hairy, round stems up to 60cm high.

LEAVES Clover has trifoliate leaves which usually come in threes, though it does vary on rare occasions. The 2cm-long ovate leaves are slightly pointy, hairy/toothed, and have a white chevron marking in the centre. The leaves are food for moths and butterflies.

FLOWERS Hermaphrodite, red/purple, dense balls of fragrant flowers are borne between two leaves. The flowers remain vertical when awaiting fertilization and will droop when they have been fertilized by a visiting bee.

SEEDS Its smooth-coated, kidney-shaped seeds are up to 2mm long and vary in colour such as tan, brown, red, yellow and green. The seeds are an important food source for birds. Seeds ripen from July–October.

LAUNCH SEEDBOMBS In spring or late summer when there is sufficient soil moisture for seed germination.

GERMINATION TIME 1–14 days.

HARVESTING SEEDS Harvest the seeds when the flower heads have turned black (30 days after full bloom).

PLANT CARE Clover requires little attention to grow vigorously. Thrives on most well-drained soils and can tolerate nutritionally poor soil. Plant in an open sunny spot. Clover suffers in heavy shade and in maritime conditions. Overwatering could cause the plant to rot.

PESTS AND DISEASES Slugs will destroy clover seedlings, and red clover mites and clover rot are a threat.

CULINARY AND MEDICINAL USES
The leaves can be added to soups, salads and as a garnish. Red clover tea helps calm stomachs, coughs, nerves and sickness and relaxes the muscles. Add 1 tbsp of fresh or dry flowers to a cup of boiling water, brew for 10 minutes and add honey. Red clover has many nutrients including vitamin C, calcium, copper, zinc, magnesium, niacin, phosphorous, potassium, thiamine and chromium and is rich in isoflavones.

OTHER USES Red clover ointments have been used to treat skin complaints.

NOTE Avoid gathering from agricultural land as it may have been treated with herbicides.

FAMILY
Leguminosae

NATIVE TO
Europe, western Asia and north-west Africa

HEIGHT/SPREAD
10–45 x 60cm

HABITAT
Roadsides, railways, waste ground, fields, rough ground and meadows

THRIVES IN
Sun/partial shade (suffers in full shade); tolerates strong winds but suffers from maritime exposure

SOIL
Thrives on chalky soils but will grow in most soil types; requires moisture

LIFESPAN
Hardy perennial herb

FLOWERS
May–September

FORM
Sprawling clumps

LEAF FORM
Trifoliate with a white V-shaped chevron on each leaf

POLLINATED BY
Bees

NOTE
Food for wildlife and livestock

CONSERVATION STATUS
No threats or conservation issues

Lady's Bedstraw

Galium verum

The common name was given because historically it was used as bedding for its coumarin scent, which combated sleeplessness and repelled fleas. It's related to Cleavers and is a good groundcover plant for neglected areas. Noted for attracting wildlife, it is a foodplant for caterpillars, bees and birds.

FAMILY
Rubiaceae

NATIVE TO
Europe, Asia

HEIGHT/SPREAD
60 x 100cm

HABITAT
Roadsides, railways, waste ground, fields; can tolerate maritime exposure

THRIVES IN
Full sun/partial shade/ deep shade

SOIL
Grows on most moist, well-drained soils (suffers on very acid soils)

LIFESPAN
Hardy perennial

FLOWERS
July–August

FORM
Creeping

LEAF FORM
Lanceolate

POLLINATED BY
Flies, beetles

NOTE
No known hazards

CONSERVATION STATUS
No known conservation issues

STEMS Wiry, square upright stems.
LEAVES Star-like whorls of 6–8 thread-like, 1–3cm-long, shiny dark green narrow leaves with a downy underside.
FLOWERS Dense clusters of tiny four-petalled honey-scented hermaphrodite flowers.
SEEDS Two ovate acid-green fruits are formed.
LAUNCH SEEDBOMBS Autumn.
GERMINATION TIME 3–4 months; slow because they need a period of cold to break dormancy.
HARVESTING SEEDS August–September.
PLANT CARE The plant can be divided throughout the season so long as it is kept moist.
PESTS AND DISEASES Generally pest- and disease-free.
CULINARY AND MEDICINAL USES The leaves are edible and added to salads. The seed is roasted as a coffee substitute and the flowering tops are distilled to make refreshing drinks. A yellow dye is obtained from the stem and used as a food colouring. Flowers are used to coagulate milk. Lady's bedstraw has a long history of use in herbal medicine though it doesn't feature much as a contemporary medicinal plant. It has been used as a diuretic and to help treat skin complaints.

Ox-eye Daisy

Leucanthemum vulgare

Ox-eye daisy is an attractive grassland perennial. It will pretty much grow anywhere except waterlogged sites. The plant has a bitter, pungent juice that deters insect pests. Ox-eye daisy planted by the house is said to repel flies.

FAMILY
Compositae/Asteraceae

NATIVE TO
Europe, Asia

HEIGHT/SPREAD
90 x 30cm

HABITAT
Roadsides, railways, waste ground, riversides, fields

THRIVES IN
Full sun/partial shade (suffers in deep shade)

SOIL
Grows on most moist soils

LIFESPAN
Hardy perennial herb

FLOWERS
May–September

FORM
Upright, clump-forming

LEAF FORM
Spatulate

POLLINATED BY
Bees, flies, beetles, Lepidoptera

NOTE
No known hazards

CONSERVATION STATUS
No known conservation issues

STEMS Stout central stem, occasionally branching, and can be slightly hairy and angular or furrowed.

LEAVES Small clump of basal, dark green, spoon-spatula-shaped, roughly toothed leaves, from which the central stem rises.

FLOWERS Hermaphrodite. Each composite flower is composed of hundreds of tiny flowers or 'florets'.

SEEDS Each floret on a flower head produces an oblongoid dark achene, 1–2mm long with up to ten light furrows. Each flower head produces up to 200 seeds.

LAUNCH SEEDBOMBS Any time. With adequate moisture, seeds will germinate continuously throughout the season.

GERMINATION TIME 1–2 weeks.

HARVESTING SEEDS August–September.

PLANT CARE More dependent on seed for regeneration than on vegetative propagation. Cut stems down to the ground in winter to promote healthy spring growth.

PESTS AND DISEASES Generally pest-free but susceptible to stem rot, verticillium wilt and leaf spots.

CULINARY AND MEDICINAL USES
The leaves are eaten in salads in Italy. The root is edible and can be eaten raw. The flower petals can be used as garnishes. Throughout the ages many medicinal uses have been derived from ox-eye daisy. The whole plant has been used to help to treat whooping cough, asthma, night sweats, ulcers, conjunctivitis and skin ailments like cuts and bruises.

Marigold

Calendula officinalis

Marigold has been valued for many centuries for its healing powers and is one of the earliest cultivated medicinal flowers. The latter part of its Latin name, 'officinalis', is the botanical term meaning 'used in the practice of medicine'. Marigold is still a popular garden plant to this day.

FAMILY
Compositae/Asteraceae

NATIVE TO
Europe

HEIGHT/SPREAD
30 x 20cm

HABITAT
Roadsides, railways, waste ground, arable land and cultivated beds

THRIVES IN
Full sun/partial shade

SOIL
Grows on most well-drained moist soils; tolerates poor soils

LIFESPAN
Hardy perennial (grown as an annual)

FLOWERS
May–October

FORM
Upright

LEAF FORM
Spatulate or oblanceolate

POLLINATED BY
Bees

NOTE
No known hazards

CONSERVATION STATUS
No known conservation issues

STEMS Marigold has stout, upright, angular branched stems, which are pale green and covered in fine hairs.

LEAVES Alternate light green, covered in fine hairs, with widely spaced teeth.

FLOWERS The bright orange or yellow monoecious daisy-like flowers are borne on a crown-shaped green receptacle. As the flower dies and petals drop off, a circular seed head remains.

SEEDS There is no seed pod; the achene (seeds) are closely curled inwards in the middle of what was the flower head. They are bent/curved, resembling a cat's claws; light brown when dry; spiky, woody and around 5–10mm long.

LAUNCH SEEDBOMBS March–April.

GERMINATION TIME 1–2 weeks.

HARVESTING SEEDS The seeds ripen for collection throughout the growing season from August–November.

PLANT CARE They require very little cultivation apart from the odd thinning out and weeding around them for tidiness. To encourage bushiness and more flowers, pinch out the growing tips. Marigolds will self-seed readily and grow pretty much anywhere. Deadhead to prevent the plant from becoming invasive. Irrigate regularly during dry periods.

PESTS AND DISEASES Suffers attacks from slugs and aphids. Susceptible to powdery mildew.

CULINARY AND MEDICINAL USES The flowers and leaves are edible. Collect flower heads or petals, dry in a dark place, then seal in an airtight container. They can be used to flavour and colour a variety of foods .The petals can be used in an edible flower salad or as a garnish. Many herbalists value marigold/ calendula for its excellent skin-healing properties and many lotions and ointments are made from it for its antiseptic, antibacterial, antiviral, antifungal and anti-inflammatory properties. They are used to help treat ailments such as nappy rash, eczema, sunburn, herpes, ulcers, chicken pox, shingles, cuts and grazes and athlete's foot and to soothe irritated nipples.

OTHER USES The petals can be made into a nourishing skin cream. A yellow dye is obtained from the flowers to dye fabrics and cosmetics. A petal infusion can be used to lighten and brighten hair. The oil has been used in perfumeries.

Feverfew

Tanacetum parthenium

This strongly scented short-lived perennial herb was historically grown for its medicinal properties. It spreads rapidly and will grow in some areas where other plants struggle. The dried flower buds can be used as an insecticide.

FAMILY
Asteraceae

NATIVE TO
South-eastern Europe, Asia

HEIGHT/SPREAD
46 x 45cm

HABITAT
Roadsides, railways, waste ground, fields, cultivated gardens and walls

THRIVES IN
Full sun
(suffers in deep shade)

SOIL
Drought tolerant; grows on most soils but thrives on free-draining sandy soils (suffers on wet soils)

LIFESPAN
Hardy perennial herb

FLOWERS
July–October

FORM
Bushy

LEAF FORM
Bipinnatifid

POLLINATED BY
Bees and flies

NOTE
Not recommended during pregnancy or for children under 2 years

CONSERVATION STATUS
No known conservation issues

STEMS Upright, branching, finely furrowed and hairy stems.

LEAVES Alternate yellow-green leaves, ferny foliage with a citrusy aroma and a downy velvety texture.

FLOWERS The flowers are hermaphrodite, daisy-like with white rays/petals and flat yellow centres and a sweet honey scent.

SEEDS The seed head is a composition of tiny fine-ridged sandy-coloured seeds.

LAUNCH SEEDBOMBS February–March.

GERMINATION TIME 1–2 weeks.

HARVESTING SEEDS Harvest when the petals have dropped and the seed head browns.

PLANT CARE Cutting back to the ground in the autumn improves the shape of the plant. Self-seeds prolifically; to manage this you may need to deadhead regularly.

PESTS AND DISEASES Can suffer attacks from aphids, chrysanthemum nematode, leaf miners, snails and slugs.

CULINARY AND MEDICINAL USES Feverfew has a bitter taste but the leaves and flowers are used as flavouring in savoury pastries, beer and soups. Feverfew has been used for assisting with menstrual pain, migraine headaches, arthritis, fevers and coughs and to aid digestion.

Bergamot/Bee Balm

Monarda didyma

This clump-forming, easy-to-grow plant, which spreads by running underground stems, has dark green leaves and impressive shaggy blooms, which will flower continuously throughout the season if deadheaded periodically. It is a good companion plant because it attracts pollinators.

FAMILY
Lamiaceae

NATIVE TO
North-eastern US

HEIGHT/SPREAD
90 x 40cm

HABITAT
Roadsides, railways, waste ground, fields, woodland, cultivated beds

THRIVES IN
Partial shade/deep shade

SOIL
Grows on most soils but thrives on acid clay soils

LIFESPAN
Hardy perennial herb

FLOWERS
June–September

FORM
Clump-forming

LEAF FORM
Ovate, spear-shaped

POLLINATED BY
Bees

NOTE
Avoid during pregnancy

CONSERVATION STATUS
No known conservation issues

STEMS Square-stemmed, characteristic of the Lamiaceae family. They are upright, tough and grooved and covered in fine dense hairs.

LEAVES Leaves are dark green, oval-shaped and coarsely toothed with red leaf veins; they have fine hairs on the underside and on the topside are sparsely hairy. The leaves are aromatic and grow opposite on the stem.

FLOWERS The hermaphrodite, ragged-looking showy flower heads comprise about 30 long curving tubular flowers, 3–4cm long, above reddish bracts. The flowers come in a range of colours and shades ranging from red and mauve to white. The tubular shape of bee balm flowers makes it easy for bees to fly in to feed from the sweet nectar and pollinate the plant in the process.

SEEDS As the seeds ripen, the seed pod dries and looks honeycomb-like and button-shaped. The nutlets (seeds) are held at the bottom of the calyx on a kind of pad and when they ripen they simply roll out and onto the ground. The tiny seeds are 1–2mm long, nut-shaped and a light brown colour. It is hard to separate them from the chaff because of their size so don't worry too much.

LAUNCH SEEDBOMBS April–May.

GERMINATION TIME 10–40 days.

HARVESTING SEEDS The seeds heads are ripe and ready to harvest from August–October.

PLANT CARE Cutting back hard after flowering encourages more blooms. Propagate by division in spring or autumn.

PESTS AND DISEASES Slugs will attack this plant and it suffers from mildew if summers are hot and dry.

CULINARY AND MEDICINAL USES Steep the leaves in water to make a refreshing citrusy tea or add to normal tea. The young shoot tips, flowers and leaves can be used raw and added to salads as a garnish. The young shoots and leaves can be cooked to enhance the flavour of foods. Frequently used to aid in treating digestive disorders and sickness, and believed to act as a carminative for flatulent colic, an expectorant and a diuretic.

OTHER USES An essential oil is obtained and used in perfumery and cosmetic products such as skin and hair treatments.

Foxglove

Digitalis purpurea

The common name foxglove comes from the Anglo-Saxon 'foxes glofa', referring to the tubular flowers suggestive of the gloves of a small animal. Medieval herbalists named the flowers 'witches' thimbles'. Native to Europe, this common biennial thrives in woodland, roadsides and wasteland.

FAMILY
Scrophulariaceae

NATIVE TO
Europe

HEIGHT/SPREAD
1–2 m x 60cm

HABITAT
Roadsides, railways, woodland, wasteland, cultivated beds

THRIVES IN
Sun/partial shade/shade

SOIL
Most well-drained soils (prefers acid)

LIFESPAN
Biennial

FLOWERS
June–September

FORM
Herbaceous biennial

LEAF FORM
Lanceolate/ovate

POLLINATED BY
Bees

NOTE
All parts of the plant are poisonous

CONSERVATION STATUS
No threats or conservation issues

STEMS The foxglove stem is strong, stout and round, woolly and greyish-green.

LEAVES For the first growing season they will develop a rosette of large, oval to lanceolate, alternate, dark green, woolly, toothed leaves that grow at the base of the plant, which will die down over winter and regrow in spring. As the plant continues to develop, the leaves gradually become smaller as they grow up the tall stems.

FLOWERS In the summer of the second growing season a display of tubular bell-shaped purple/pink flowers appear with spotted maroon to purple insides. A spotty landing pad helps the bees identify where to land. The reproductive parts of the flower are positioned in the roof of the flower tunnel and as the bee travels along the tunnel, pollen sticks to its fluffy back.

SEEDS The long oval seed pod contains hundreds of dust-like reddish-brown/black seeds; one plant can produce up to 2 million seeds.

LAUNCH SEEDBOMBS June through to the end of August.

GERMINATION TIME 2–3 weeks.

HARVESTING SEEDS Collect seeds June–August when the seed pods begin to brown. It is advisable when collecting foxglove seeds to wear protective gloves to avoid any potential skin irritation and a protective mask so as not to breathe in the fine seeds as they can be an irritant.

PLANT CARE Use gloves when handling this plant, to avoid any skin irritations. Because of its tall spikes, foxglove may need staking for support if winds are high to avoid damage, which could result in broken stems and collapse. Pinch off faded flowers to prolong their flowering season; when flowering has finished, cut the stems off at the base of the plant. Foxgloves self-seed readily so you may want to thin out some of the seedlings in your garden. Water early in the day or late afternoon and feed as necessary.

PESTS AND DISEASES Foxgloves are relatively pest-free plants but do need to be planted 45cm apart and provided with adequate drainage and air circulation because they are susceptible to crown rot, leaf spot and powdery mildew.

CULINARY AND MEDICINAL USES Not edible. Foxglove is TOXIC. DO NOT USE AS A HOME HERBAL PLANT.

Sweet Cicely

Myrrhis odorata

Sweet cicely has been cultivated as a medicinal herb for centuries and has been growing wild since the 1770s. It was planted in graveyards in South Wales 'in memory of sweetness' and possibly as a myrrh substitute – it was believed that it bloomed on Christmas Eve.

STEMS The upright, round hollow stems are light green, slightly grooved and hairy, with characteristic leaf sheaths.

LEAVES Aromatic, light green, finely divided, fern-like and up to 50cm long, with slightly downy undersides; often the leaves show characteristic pale patches.

FLOWERS Umbels of flat-topped hermaphrodite clusters of tiny white flowers, each having five unequal, erratically notched white petals and protruding stamens.

SEEDS The seeds are 2cm long, shiny, ribbed and slightly hairy. They resemble seed pods but are actually seeds. The seeds can be sown green or left to ripen and turn black.

LAUNCH SEEDBOMBS July–August if freshly harvested or March–May if purchased.

GERMINATION TIME The seeds need several months of cold weather to germinate.

HARVESTING SEEDS Seeds ripen for harvesting from July–August.

PLANT CARE Sweet cicely is a low-maintenance plant and requires little attention. If the leaves are required for cooking, it is best to prevent the plant from flowering as the flowering process reduces the flavour of the foliage – but in doing so you will, of course, have no seeds for cooking with! Sweet cicely self-seeds freely. Divide the plant from September–May.

PESTS AND DISEASES Generally pest- and disease-free.

CULINARY AND MEDICINAL USES
The leaves, roots and seeds can be eaten cooked or raw and Sweet cicely is one of the dried herbs in a 'bouquet garni' herb mix. A refreshing tea is also made from the leaves. They can be added to stewed gooseberries or rhubarb to reduce the acidity (also, less sugar will be needed). They can be boiled and used as a root vegetable, or added to salads. The seeds can be ground as a spice or chopped and used to flavour salads, cream and bakery goods such as cookies, cakes and fruit pies. Sweet cicely can be used for the treatment of coughs, colds, flatulence and digestive disorders and as a gentle stimulant. The roots can be made into an ointment, which may be used to treat skin ailments and soothe wounds.

FAMILY
Umbelliferae/Apiaceae

NATIVE TO
UK and Europe

HEIGHT/SPREAD
200 x 100cm

HABITAT
Damp ditches on roadsides, railways, waste ground, streamsides, field and woodland margins, hills and mountains

THRIVES IN
Full sun/partial shade/ deep shade

SOIL
Most moist soils; tolerates heavy clay

LIFESPAN
Herbaceous perennial herb

FLOWERS
May–June

FORM
Clump-forming

LEAF FORM
Tripinnate to bipinnate

POLLINATED BY
Bees, beetles and flies

NOTE
No known hazards

CONSERVATION STATUS
No known conservation issues

Lemon Balm

Melissa officinalis

Lemon balm is a commonly grown plant used as a household remedy; it has traditionally been made into a tonic to lift the spirits. The Latin name for lemon balm, 'Melissa', is Greek for honey bee; the bees love to feed from the nectar-rich flowers, which appear throughout the summer.

FAMILY
Labiatae

NATIVE TO
Europe, Asia, North Africa

HEIGHT/SPREAD
100 x 40cm

HABITAT
Roadsides, railways, waste ground, cultivated beds

THRIVES IN
Full sun/partial shade

SOIL
Drought tolerant, grows on most well-drained soils

LIFESPAN
Hardy perennial herb

FLOWERS
June–October

FORM
Upright, bushy

LEAF FORM
Ovate

POLLINATED BY
Bees

NOTE
Not recommended for those taking thyroid medication

CONSERVATION STATUS
No known conservation issues

STEMS Wiry, square-branched upright stems.

LEAVES The green lemon-scented broad leaves are serrated and grow opposite each other up the stem.

FLOWERS The flowers are nectar-full hermaphrodite, 1.3cm long, white tubular in shape with two lips.

SEEDS 1mm long, smooth, black and oval-shaped.

LAUNCH SEEDBOMBS April and September.

GERMINATION TIME 1–3 weeks.

HARVESTING SEEDS The seed heads are ripe for harvest August–October.

PLANT CARE Regularly trimming will promote fresh young leaf growth and prevent vigorous spreading. To keep foliage flavoursome, cut back some of the flowering stems but leave a few for the bees to enjoy. Divide in spring or autumn and take cuttings in July/August. It will self-sow readily from seed and can be propagated by taking stem cuttings, which will root easily if placed in a jar of water. Can be invasive as it grows quickly and spreads easily. A way of tackling this in small cultivated beds is to grow it in a pot and sink the pot into the ground. Lemon balm requires regular watering but does not require any feeding.

PESTS AND DISEASES Relatively pest-free. Can suffer from verticillium wilt and mint rust.

CULINARY AND MEDICINAL USES The leaves are the main edible parts used for their lemon aroma and flavour; they can be eaten raw or cooked. Lemon balm can be used to flavour soups, salads, sauces, poultry stuffings and vegetables, beverages like tea and iced and alcoholic drinks. Lemon balm has been long used because of its antibacterial and antiviral properties to help treat digestive problems, coughs, colds and flu, menstrual cramps and toothache, for dressing wounds and, according to studies, to calm the nerves and soothe tension. In the Middles Ages it was used as a cure-all plant to treat skin eruptions and cricked necks and to relieve morning sickness.

OTHER USES Even after harvesting, the leaves and flowers have a long-lasting aroma and can be used as a potpourri. The crushed leaves rubbed on the skin can be used as a mosquito repellent.

"I GO TO NATURE TO BE SOOTHED
AND HEALED, AND TO HAVE MY
SENSES PUT IN ORDER."

John Burroughs

Borage

Borago officinalis

The whole plant is covered in white prickly hairs and has a messy straggling shape. Its star-shaped flowers attract throngs of busy bees.

<table>
<tr><td>FAMILY
Boraginaceae</td></tr>
<tr><td>NATIVE TO
Europe, North Africa</td></tr>
<tr><td>HEIGHT/SPREAD
60 x 80cm</td></tr>
<tr><td>HABITAT
Disturbed ground, roadsides, railways, waste ground, cultivated beds</td></tr>
<tr><td>THRIVES IN
Full sun/partial shade</td></tr>
<tr><td>SOIL
Grows on most soils (can tolerate nutritionally poor soil)</td></tr>
<tr><td>LIFESPAN
Hardy annual</td></tr>
<tr><td>FLOWERS
June–October</td></tr>
<tr><td>FORM
Upright, straggling</td></tr>
<tr><td>LEAF FORM
Ovate to lanceolate</td></tr>
<tr><td>POLLINATED BY
Bees</td></tr>
<tr><td>NOTE
The leaves, not the oil, contain small traces of pyrrolizidine alkaloids that may cause liver damage</td></tr>
<tr><td>CONSERVATION STATUS
No known conservation issues</td></tr>
</table>

STEMS Stout, bristly branched, hollow round stems.

LEAVES The leaves alternate ovate to lanceolate, deep green and wrinkled.

FLOWERS Clusters of hairy flower buds, which open into deep blue star-shaped flowers; the corolla consists of five spreading, purplish lanceolate lobes.

SEEDS The seed forms throughout the growing season and consists of four black ribbed nutlets.

LAUNCH SEEDBOMBS Any time.

GERMINATION TIME 1–2 weeks.

HARVESTING SEEDS Collect seeds when ripe.

PLANT CARE Borage will seed itself freely and comes up year after year, so it may be prudent to collect some of the seeds before the plant takes over. It is common for plants to show signs of mildew when grown in dry conditions. May need protection from wind.

PESTS AND DISEASES Foliage attacked by slugs and leaf miners. Powdery mildew.

CULINARY AND MEDICINAL USES Has a cucumber flavour and fragrance. The flowers and leaves are edible. An infusion may help to treat fevers, chest colds, mouth ulcers, sore throats and menstrual problems. Externally it helps to treat inflammatory swellings, itches, sore eyes and skin conditions.

Wild Chives

Allium schoenoprasum

Chives are a common garden plant cultivated for their strongly flavoured edible leaves. They are clump-forming and are ideal for edging beds and paths or letting naturalize randomly. Chives attract wildlife, especially bees and butterflies.

FAMILY
Alliaceae

NATIVE TO
Europe, Asia, North America

HEIGHT/SPREAD
45 x 15cm

HABITAT
Roadsides, railways, waste ground, woodland garden, cultivated beds

THRIVES IN
Full sun/partial shade

SOIL
Most soil types (prefers poor soil); drought tolerant

LIFESPAN
Hardy perennial bulb herb

FLOWERS
July–August

FORM
Spiky, spreading

LEAF FORM
Strap-like, tubular, hollow

POLLINATED BY
Long-tongued insects like butterflies, moths and bees

NOTE
No known hazards

CONSERVATION STATUS
No known conservation issues

STEMS Narrow hollow stems sprout from the bulb.

LEAVES Chives have hollow, tubular, bright green leaves with a pleasant onion flavour.

FLOWERS The flowers are hermaphrodite mauve/purple and resemble a pompom. Each flower head is a composition of multiples of tiny flowers.

SEEDS Each tiny flower produces its own papery seed pod, each containing six pointy 2mm black seeds.

LAUNCH SEEDBOMBS March to April.

GERMINATION TIME 1–3 weeks.

HARVESTING SEEDS Harvest seeds when the flowers are spent.

PLANT CARE Regular harvesting gives a continuous supply of young leaves. To encourage fresh new growth, clumps can be divided in spring.

PESTS AND DISEASES Relatively pest- and disease-free.

CULINARY AND MEDICINAL USES
The flowers and leaves of chives have a mild onion flavour and can be used for flavouring salads, for Asian dishes, soups, cheeses and dips. Try adding chives to a salad of home-grown potatoes. Take a pair of scissors and the salad bowl straight to the plant and cut off the leaves/flowers, snipping to the length required in situ. The whole plant is believed to be beneficial for the digestive system and blood circulation.

Wild Marjoram

Origanum vulgare

Primarily grown as a pot herb, this woody, sprawling, upright, bushy perennial with aromatic, flavoursome foliage is used for culinary and medicinal purposes. Wild marjoram makes a good companion plant for vegetables and other herbs.

FAMILY
Lamiaceae

NATIVE TO
Europe, Asia

HEIGHT/SPREAD
45 x 45cm

HABITAT
Roadsides, railways, waste ground, arable land, cultivated beds

THRIVES IN
Full sun
(suffers in deep shade)

SOIL
Drought tolerant; grows on most soils but thrives on free-draining sandy soils

LIFESPAN
Hardy perennial herb

FLOWERS
July–September

FORM
Sprawling

LEAF FORM
Ovate

POLLINATED BY
Long-tongued insects like butterflies, moths and bees

NOTE
Its oil may cause skin irritation. It is not recommended during pregnancy

CONSERVATION STATUS
Is not threatened and is a commonly cultivated plant

STEMS Like all plants in the *Lamiaceae* family, wild marjoram has distinctive square stems, which are slightly purple and downy.

LEAVES Its flavoursome, aromatic, dark green leaves are 2.5cm long, ovate, slightly toothed and borne opposite on the stem.

FLOWERS The dark purple buds at the top of purplish stems open to reveal dense, rose-pink clusters of tiny tubular hermaphrodite flowers.

SEEDS The 0.5mm-long seeds are egg-shaped and rusty in colour, with a smooth testa.

LAUNCH SEEDBOMBS At any time of the year, but the best results are probably achieved from an autumn sowing.

GERMINATION TIME 1–2 weeks.

HARVESTING SEEDS The seeds ripen from August to October and are ready to harvest when the seed heads are dry on the plant.

PLANT CARE Wild marjoram is a great colonizer of sparsely vegetated ground. Its long roots have numerous root hairs, which enable the absorption of subsoil water in periods of drought. Can be grown in pots on a sunny patio.

PESTS AND DISEASES The aromatic quality of wild marjoram deters pests. Seldom attacked by diseases, but to prevent risks ensure that air can circulate freely by planting evenly spaced.

CULINARY AND MEDICINAL USES Wild marjoram has been used as a culinary and medicinal herb for thousands of years. The leaves have a fuller flavour just before the plant flowers and can be clipped fresh or dried and added to salad dressings, vegetables or chillies. The flowers can be eaten sprinkled over salads or mixed in a potato salad. Wild marjoram leaves and flowering stems can be made into a refreshing tea when steeped in boiling water for 20 minutes, strained and served with honey to taste. A mild tea is believed to help alleviate menstrual pains and promote a restful night's sleep. Wild marjoram is thought to help promote menstruation, act as an antiseptic, and have beneficial effects on the digestive and respiratory systems.

NOTE Wild marjoram has strong sedative effects and should be consumed in small doses. It is not recommended as a safe plant to be used during pregnancy.

Wild Mint

Mentha arvensis

Wild mint has fresh fragrant foliage (though not as pungent as other mints); the scent becomes more apparent when the leaves are brushed past or bruised. Mint has been cultivated for its culinary and medicinal properties since ancient times, and has been found in Egyptian tombs dating back to 1000 BC.

FAMILY
Labiatae

NATIVE TO
Europe and Asia

HEIGHT/SPREAD
50 x 100cm

HABITAT
Roadsides, railways, waste ground, fields, cultivated beds

THRIVES IN
Full sun/partial shade

SOIL
Grows on most moist soils and will grow in heavy clay soil

LIFESPAN
Hardy perennial herb

FLOWERS
May–October

FORM
Creeping rhizomes

LEAF FORM
Ovate, lanceolate

POLLINATED BY
Insects, bees

NOTE
Not recommended during pregnancy

CONSERVATION STATUS
No known conservation issues

STEMS Upright, tough, hollow, square, slightly hairy, green-purplish branching stems (adventitious roots may sprout from lower nodes).

LEAVES Opposite, short-stalked, narrowly ovate, sharply toothed, hairy.

FLOWERS The flowers are formed in compact clusters of separate whorls, which are borne in the middle and upper leaf axils. Five united hairy sepals surround the funnel-shaped hermaphrodite flowers. The flowers are pink/purple, 4–7mm long, with five united petals consisting of two upper and three lower lobes; there are two long and three short stamens. The flower matures into a capsule containing four nutlets (seeds).

SEEDS The seeds are tan-coloured, glabrous, oval-shaped and 1mm long. Growing wild mint from seed is very variable and it might be that the flowers and shape are not uniform.

LAUNCH SEEDBOMBS April–October.

GERMINATION TIME 1 week.

HARVESTING SEEDS The seed heads ripen between July and October.

PLANT CARE Wild mint has rather aggressive spreading roots and if you want to prevent them from roaming, restrain them by planting in a container and sink it into the soil. Division can be easily carried out at almost any time of the year, though there will be more success in spring or autumn. Cut back in the autumn. Water regularly.

PESTS AND DISEASES Seldom attacked by pests. May suffer from mint rust.

CULINARY AND MEDICINAL USES The leaves of wild mint can be eaten raw or cooked to be used in salads, cooked foods, desserts, hot and cold beverages and as a garnish. Add mint to a tasty hedgerow fruit salad using foraged plants such as blackberries and wild strawberries. Wild mint is valued for its beneficial effects on digestion and its antiseptic, anaesthetic, antispasmodic and aromatic properties. It has agents in it that can help neutralize inflammation and relieve fevers, colds, headaches, diarrhoea and stomach pains. Fresh leaves can be chewed and inserted into the nostrils to relieve cold symptoms.

OTHER USES The plant is used as an insect and vermin repellent, and to deodorize houses. An essential oil is obtained from the plant, which is used in products worldwide.

Fennel

Foeniculum vulgare

Fennel grows naturally over most of Europe; it spread to India and was introduced to the USA in the 1800s. In the UK it grows wild in the south of England and North Wales along the coastal areas. Fennel is widely cultivated for its strong-flavoured leaves and seeds.

FAMILY
Umbelliferae /Apiaceae

NATIVE TO
Europe/naturalized in the UK

HEIGHT/SPREAD
150 x 100cm

HABITAT
Roadsides, railways, waste ground, fields, maritime, cultivated beds

THRIVES IN
Full sun
(suffers in deep shade)

SOIL
Drought tolerant; grows on most fertile moist soils but prefers calcareous soil

LIFESPAN
Evergreen perennial herb

FLOWERS
August–October

FORM
Upright, feathery

LEAF FORM
Tripinnate

POLLINATED BY
Insects

NOTE
The sap or essential oil has been noted to cause photo-sensitivity

CONSERVATION STATUS
No known conservation issues

STEMS Upright, branching, hollow, glaucous-green stems hold alternate leaves and terminate with 5–25cm-wide umbelliferous flower heads.

LEAVES The leaves are composed of long, finely dissected, threadlike, green/blue soft feathery aromatic leaflets.

FLOWERS Large flat umbels of yellow hermaphrodite flowers. The umbels consist of 20 to 50 tiny flowers on short pedicels.

SEEDS 4–10mm-long, grooved, compressed, olive/brown seeds, which are released through openings when the seed pod dries.

LAUNCH SEEDBOMBS March–April.

GERMINATION TIME 2–3 weeks.

HARVESTING SEEDS The seed heads ripen from September to October.

PLANT CARE Fennel tolerates drought but that's not to say it wouldn't like a regular soaking over dry periods. As it can grow to such a height, fennel will need to be sheltered from strong winds. Cut back the old growth in winter months. Fennel can be container-grown in a pot no smaller than 40cm wide and 30cm deep. To ensure good growth for culinary harvesting, feed every month with a liquid fertilizer.

PESTS AND DISEASES Can suffer slug and aphid attacks. Usually disease-free.

CULINARY AND MEDICINAL USES Fennel is a herb used worldwide in traditional cooking. The edible parts are the root, stem, leaves, pollen and seed. Fennel is a strong, aromatic and flavoursome herb. It can be used to make a herbal tea with a calming and antispasmodic effect, which aids digestive cramps. Fennel can be found in many forms. The dried seeds have a strong anise flavour; the pollen is the most potent and most expensive form of fennel and is 100 times stronger and sweeter than the seed. It is added as a spice to vegetables and roast meat dishes. The leaves have a delicate flavour and can be added to salads, fish soups and sauces. The bulb is crisp and treated as a root vegetable, which can be eaten raw or sautéed, stewed, grilled or braised. Fennel is one of the primary ingredients of absinthe. In India, fennel seeds are eaten raw and are said to improve eyesight. Fennel is said to improve milk production in nursing mothers and can also be used to treat chronic coughs, colds, flu, bad breath and constipation, and is used as a diuretic.

Common Thyme

Thymus vulgaris

It was once believed that fairies lived in patches of thyme and historical gardeners would set aside a patch for them! Thyme is one of the most commonly known herbs and there is never a herb garden without one or a kitchen cupboard without a pot of the dried herb.

STEMS Gnarled, woody, many-branched stem holding opposite paired leaves.
LEAVES The upper of the leaf is dark green and the underside is grey and downy. The leaf margins are distinctively rolled under.
FLOWERS The tips of the branches hold clustered whorls of hermaphrodite lilac-pinkish-purple tubular two-lipped flowers.
SEEDS Small, globular and brown/black in colour.
LAUNCH SEEDBOMBS March–April and September–October.
GERMINATION TIME 3–4 weeks.
HARVESTING SEEDS The seed will ripen for harvesting from July–September.
PLANT CARE Thyme can get very woody and the foliage sparse; to prevent this, cut back after flowering. Leaves can be harvested for fresh use throughout the summer, but the flavour is best just before flowering. Once plants are established, prune regularly and remove dead flowers and old wood. Protect from harsh weather conditions, especially wet, by adding a layer of gravel around their bases. Thyme can be propagated by root cuttings, softwood cuttings, semi-hardwood cuttings, division and layering, as well as by seed. When you maintain the health of your plant, use it as part of your harvesting routine; the leaves can be used fresh or dried and stored for later use.
PESTS AND DISEASES Generally pest-free. Thyme can get root rot if waterlogged.
CULINARY AND MEDICINAL USES The leaves can be used fresh or dry. Thyme goes with whatever you team it with, from stews, soups and sauces to meat, fish and vegetable dishes. Thyme is an important ingredient of the herb mix 'bouquet garni'. Thymol is what gives thyme leaves their strong flavour; its medicinal properties are used to treat dental problems and sore gums and it is a main ingredient for mouthwashes. A herbal tea can be prepared to help treat coughs, whooping cough, asthma, colds and flus. Add 2 teaspoons of dried herb per cup of boiling water and steep for 10 minutes. An antiseptic essential oil is derived from thyme which may help treat depression, fatigue, headache, muscular pains and respiratory problems and to make cough medicines. The oil can also be added to a carrier oil to be used as a chest rub, applied to bites and wounds, or added to the bath.

FAMILY
Lamiaceae

NATIVE TO
Europe

HEIGHT/SPREAD
20 x 30cm

HABITAT
Rocky hillsides, roadsides, railways, waste ground, cultivated beds

THRIVES IN
Full sun
(suffers in the shade)

SOIL
Drought tolerant; grows on sandy, alkaline, neutral, free-draining soils

LIFESPAN
Evergreen subshrub

FLOWERS
June–August

FORM
Woody, ground cover

LEAF FORM
Ovate-lanceolate

POLLINATED BY
Butterflies, moths, bees, flies

NOTE
Essential oil (thymol) derived from plant is toxic if ingested

CONSERVATION STATUS
No known conservation issues

Common Sorrel

Rumex acetosa

Cultivated as a pot herb in Europe until the Middle Ages but now seen as a wild foodplant noted for attracting wildlife such as Lepidoptera and birds. Because they contain oxalic acid, sorrel leaves have a tangy citrus flavour, making them a popular choice for salads and soups.

FAMILY
Polygonaceae

NATIVE TO
Europe

HEIGHT/SPREAD
60 x 30cm

HABITAT
Roadsides, railways, waste land, meadows, cultivated beds, cliffs and coastal dunes

THRIVES IN
Full sun/partial shade

SOIL
Drought tolerant; grows on most moist soils but prefers acid soil

LIFESPAN
Perennial herb

FLOWERS
May–June

FORM
Spreading

LEAF FORM
Oblong heart-shaped

POLLINATED BY
Wind

NOTE
Contains oxalic acid, potentially toxic if ingested in large doses

CONSERVATION STATUS
No known conservation issues

STEMS Reddish-green, glabrous (hairless), slightly grooved stem with a papery sheath at the base of each leaf.

LEAVES The oblong-heart-shaped leaves, almost acid green in colour, have characteristic pointed basal lobes that direct backwards.

FLOWERS Spikes of inconspicuous reddish-green dioecious flower (and later seed) clusters grow above the leaves.

SEEDS Three-sided, pointed at each end, glossy dark brown/red, 3mm long achene (2,000 seeds are produced per plant).

LAUNCH SEEDBOMBS Any time.

GERMINATION TIME 1–2 weeks.

HARVESTING SEEDS June–August.

PLANT CARE For culinary purposes, cut back the flowering stalks in July so the plant can use its energy for leaf production rather than flower production. Water during the summer months and protect from frosts.

PESTS AND DISEASES Generally pest- and disease-free.

CULINARY AND MEDICINAL USES The young leaves and stem are best eaten raw in salads and the older leaves can be used for soups. Used to help treat sore throats and sinusitis; diuretic and a cooling drink for fevers.

OTHER USES A grey-blue dye can be obtained from the leaves and stems. Makes an interesting dried flower in arrangements and bouquets.

Coltsfoot

Tussilago farfara

Coltsfoot is seen as a common invasive weed, which grows abundantly on wasteland and neglected sites by rivers and the seaside. Dandelion-like flowers emerge first and when the seed head forms and the stem dies, hoof-shaped leaves begin to appear.

FAMILY
Asteraceae/Compositae

NATIVE TO
Europe and Asia

HEIGHT/SPREAD
30 x 100cm

HABITAT
Roadsides, railways, waste ground, maritime, arable fields

THRIVES IN
Full sun/partial shade/ deep shade

SOIL
Grows on most moist, free-draining soils; thrives on acid soils

LIFESPAN
Hardy, rhizomatous herbaceous perennial

FLOWERS
March–April

FORM
Creeping, clump-forming

LEAF FORM
Hoof-shaped

POLLINATED BY
Insects, wind

NOTE
The plant contains traces of pyrrolizidine alkaloids, which if ingested in large doses can be potentially toxic to the liver

CONSERVATION STATUS
No known conservation issues

STEMS It has upright, unbranched, downy stems, which are covered with alternate reddish-brown scales and terminate in one flower bud.

LEAVES The long-stalked, dark green leaves have grey downy undersides (the young leaves are downy on both sides) and are round-hoof-shaped with slightly toothed edges, divided into five to 12 lobes. The leaves sprout from the rhizome when the flowers and seeds are spent. The leaves can be collected, chopped up and dried between May and July.

FLOWERS Its single-rowed involucre is composed of around 300 yellow strap-like ray florets and around 40 tubular disc florets followed by the seed head, which is a white downy globe.

SEEDS The seeds are 1mm cylindrical glabrous achenes, which occur in the outer ray florets and, rarely, the inner disc florets. They have a feathery plume to aid wind dispersal and can travel distances of over 4km. The number of seeds per seed head is around 160.

LAUNCH SEEDBOMBS March–April or September.

GERMINATION TIME 1–2 weeks.

HARVESTING SEEDS Seeds will ripen for harvesting from April–June.

PLANT CARE Coltsfoot can be a problem weed in cultivated gardens; to control spread, cut off flowering heads before they set seed and remove leaves to will exhaust the rhizomes. It can be planted in a sunken container to prevent spread in a cultivated bed. Divide rhizomes any time in the year and plant the divisions straight into their permanent positions.

PESTS AND DISEASES Slugs attack the flowers, and the rhizomes fall prey to wireworms, swift moth larvae and cockchafers. Seldom attacked by diseases.

CULINARY AND MEDICINAL USES The flowers can be gathered and dried from March–April and the leaves from May–July or the leaves can be used fresh until autumn. Young flowers and buds can be eaten raw or cooked in soups; burnt leaves are used to season foods. Do not exceed 10g of coltsfoot per day. Historically used as a relaxant, expectorant, demulcent and diuretic.

Anise/Aniseed

Pimpinella anisum

Anise is known as a cultivated crop but it also grows wild. It is in the same family as carrot and parsley. Its aromatic qualities make anise good companion plants and a pest deterrent, while also attracting parasitic wasps to prey on pests.

FAMILY
Umbelliferae

NATIVE TO
Middle East, Egypt, Greece, Europe

HEIGHT/SPREAD
60 x 40cm

HABITAT
More suited to cultivated beds but can grow in wild situations too

THRIVES IN
Full sun
(suffers in deep shade)

SOIL
Grows in most moist, free-draining soils

LIFESPAN
Annual herb

FLOWERS
July–August

FORM
Feathery, delicate

LEAF FORM
Lower: Heart-shaped;
Upper: Pinnate

POLLINATED BY
Insects

NOTE
Not recommended during pregnancy

CONSERVATION STATUS
No known conservation issues

STEMS Slender, round, grooved stems branch off at the top.

LEAVES The lower leaves are round to heart-shaped and coarsely toothed, whereas the upper leaves are pinnate, divided, delicately feathery and bright green.

FLOWERS Clusters of tiny yellow/white self-fertile umbelliferae flowers develop.

SEEDS The brown fruit is a downy, flattened ovate and contains two brown ribbed seeds with a liquorice flavour.

LAUNCH SEEDBOMBS March and September.

GERMINATION TIME Up to 3 weeks.

HARVESTING SEEDS Fruits ripen July–September.

PLANT CARE Protect the plants from winds with support (the seed heads can become quite heavy and pull the plant down). Ensure it is positioned in full sunshine to promote healthy growth. Water regularly when hot and during dry weather (always water plants in the morning or the evening).

PESTS AND DISEASES Generally pest-free but susceptible to rust, downy mildew and powdery mildew.

CULINARY AND MEDICINAL USES The seeds are used to flavour liqueur and confectioneries. Anise tea may help to treat coughs, pectoral problems and menstrual cramps; it is carminative, antidepressant, antifungal and aids digestion.

Liquorice

Glycyrrhiza glabra

Liquorice is a robust, woody-stemmed herbaceous perennial with feathery foliage and purplish/blue to white flower spikes. A slow-growing plant that becomes more productive as a root crop after three years of growth.

FAMILY
Fabaceae or Leguminosae

NATIVE TO
Mediterranean and Asia

HEIGHT/SPREAD
100x100 cm

HABITAT
Dry open places, thrives in a maritime climate

THRIVES IN
Full sun

SOIL
Most, moist well drained soils

LIFESPAN
Perennial

FLOWERS
June–July

FORM
Herbaceous perennial with a branching root system

LEAF FORM
Imparipinnate, narrowly lanceolate leaves

POLLINATED BY
Insects

NOTE
If pregnant or have liver cirrhosis use with caution. This plant is a nitrogen fixer and can be used as a companion plant

CONSERVATION STATUS
No known conservation issues

STEMS The trailing stems are woody.

LEAVES Feathery leaves with sticky hairs; at night the leaflets droop down.

FLOWERS Hermaphrodite flowers that bloom on long stems followed by smooth-skinned pods containing three brown seeds.

LAUNCH SEEDBOMBS Spring or autumn.

GERMINATION TIME 3–6 weeks (presoaking or scarification may be required for prompt germination).

HARVESTING SEEDS July–August.

PLANT CARE May need protecting from slugs in the first few years of growth. The roots are nitrogen-fixing. Divide in autumn and plant in new location immediately.

PESTS AND DISEASES Spider mites, slugs and snails. Susceptible to powdery mildew and rust.

CULINARY AND MEDICINAL USES
Often used in confectionery manufacturing. The roots can be chewed or cut up and used to make herbal tea (1 teaspoon per cup of boiling water). Cultivated for its roots, liquorice is a widely used plant in Western herbal medicine for its medicinal properties, which can help to soothe and treat conditions such as coughs, mouth ulcers, catarrh, bronchitis and sore throats. It is may also help to relieve arthritis and for detoxifying and protecting the liver.

Self-heal

Prunella vulgaris

'Self-heal', 'heal-all', 'heart-of-the-earth' – this tiny plant is revered for its powerful properties. It was once believed that Self-heal was a holy herb, sent by God to heal all ailments of mankind and animals. Some Native American tribes drank this root tea before hunting.

FAMILY
Lamiaceae

NATIVE TO
Europe, Asia and Africa

HEIGHT/SPREAD
20 x 30cm

HABITAT
Roadsides, railways, waste ground, fields, scrubland, wooded clearings

THRIVES IN
Full sun/partial shade/ shade

SOIL
Grows on most moist, well-drained soils

LIFESPAN
Hardy perennial herb

FLOWERS
May–September

FORM
Upright, groundcover

LEAF FORM
Lanceolate

POLLINATED BY
Bees

NOTE
No known hazards

CONSERVATION STATUS
No known conservation issues

STEMS The stem is square, tough and green with reddish pinstripes running up the stem at the corners of the square, branching at the leaf axis and bearing opposite paired leaves.

LEAVES The leaves are around 10mm long and 5mm wide, lance-shaped and slightly serrated, rich green with reddish tips and short stalks.

FLOWERS The hermaphrodite flowers grow from a purplish-red club-like cluster at the top of the stem. The flowers are deep purple and tubular with two lips, the lower lip being bearded. Directly below the 'flower club' is a pair of stalkless leaves, which act as a kind of collar. After flowering, the 'club' becomes a purple-tinged seed head.

SEEDS The seeds are 3mm long, smooth, oval-shaped and rusty brown with slight furrows; when ripe they fall from the seed head and germinate in the ground around the parent plant, but can also be wind-dispersed.

LAUNCH SEEDBOMBS At any time of the year.

GERMINATION TIME Depends on when you sow them, but usually 1–4 weeks.

HARVESTING SEEDS The seeds ripen for harvest from August–September.

PLANT CARE Self-heal can be invasive and self-propagates readily by seed; to keep colonies controlled, deadhead on a regular basis – use this as part of your harvesting regime. The plant also self-propagates vegetatively through layering (when a stem makes contact with the soil it will develop roots and grow into an individual plant).

PESTS AND DISEASES Generally pest- and disease-free.

CULINARY AND MEDICINAL USES The leaves and small flowers are edible. The flowering tops can be dried to be used later; store in a cool, dry, dark place. It can be added to salads and stewed meat dishes. The whole flower 'clubs' with stem attached would make perfect stirrers for summer drinks. For tea to strengthen the immune system, add 28 g/1 oz dried or fresh herb to 600 ml/1 pint of boiling water, steep and add honey to taste. Drink in half-cup doses. Research shows that self-heal can help lower blood pressure and has antibacterial and antibiotic properties. It can be used as a diuretic.

OTHER USES Makes an olive-green dye.

Echinacea (Coneflower)

Echinacea purpurea

Echinacea was used by the Native Americans and the early settlers adopted it as a medicine. It is a fast-growing, versatile herbaceous perennial with a vigorous, long flowering season. It requires little attention once established and is an important foodplant for wildlife.

FAMILY
Compositae/Asteraceae

NATIVE TO
USA

HEIGHT/SPREAD
120 x 45cm

HABITAT
Gravelly hillsides, prairies, open woodland, cultivated beds (has been spotted on roadsides)

THRIVES IN
Full sun/partial shade (suffers in deep shade)

SOIL
Drought tolerant; grows on most moist, free-draining soils; tolerates clay

LIFESPAN
Hardy perennial herb

FLOWERS
June–September

FORM
Clump-forming, rhizomatous, upright stems

LEAF FORM
Lanceolate to ovate

POLLINATED BY
Insects

NOTE
Rare side effects possible

CONSERVATION STATUS
No known conservation issues

STEMS Stoutly round, upright fuzzy stems bear opposite medium/large leaves at the base and intermittently along the stem, almost up to the flower head.

LEAVES Pale to dark green, coarse, toothed and hairy with three prominent veins.

FLOWERS Hermaphrodite, sweet-scented pink/lavender/deep purple daisy-like ray flowers. The petals are 'reflexed' (point downwards) and surround a raised central orange/rich ochre cone.

SEEDS The seed head is dome-shaped, dense and prickly and the seeds are achenes – light brown, 5mm long and cone-shaped with ragged toothed ends.

LAUNCH SEEDBOMBS March–April.

GERMINATION TIME 2–4 weeks.

HARVESTING SEEDS Harvest seeds when the seed heads are ripe and dry – a good clue is when you spot the birds having a munch. Take some seed heads but remember to leave some for the birds as they rely on it in the colder months.

PLANT CARE Because the stems are so tough echinacea doesn't require staking. It copes well with adverse weather conditions. Cut back stems as the blooms fade to encourage further flower production. Cut back dead flower stems to the ground in autumn and feed in the spring or autumn. Water regularly, however, echinacea cannot tolerate being waterlogged. Divide the plant in spring or autumn and while you are at it you could take some root cuttings.

PESTS AND DISEASES Can suffer attacks from leaf miners and slugs. Susceptible to powdery mildew and leaf spots.

CULINARY AND MEDICINAL USES
Echinacea is commonly used to prevent colds and boost the immune system. It comes in many forms such as tonics, teas, tinctures, tablets, lotions and ointments, root powder, and in loose, dry leaf and flower form. For tea, place 2 teaspoons of dried or fresh leaves in a teapot and cover with 1 cup of boiling water. Leave to steep for 20 minutes, strain and enjoy. Historically, a very important herbal plant, which is still widely used to help alleviate a variety of ailments such as skin rashes, gynaecological problems, toothache, sore throats and colds and to boost the immune system; it may also help speed up recovery time after an infection.

*Use Echinacea with caution if you are allergic to ragweek or plants in the Asteraceae/ Compositae family as it could cause rashes and asthma attacks. However, such side effects are extremely rare, which is why Echinacea is such a widely used plant in the world of medicine.

Arnica

Arnica montana

An upright, elegant, jolly alpine plant. Highly valued since the sixteenth century for its medicinal and healing properties, which are now widely used in a range of alternative medical practices such as homeopathy and herbalism.

FAMILY
Asteraceae/Compositae

NATIVE TO
Europe, Asia,
North America

HEIGHT/SPREAD
45 x 30cm

HABITAT
Woodland, hedgerow,
pastures, cultivated beds

THRIVES IN
Full sun/partial shade

SOIL
Most moist, free-draining
soils; tolerates poor soil

LIFESPAN
Herbaceous perennial

FLOWERS
June–August

FORM
Alpine plant

LEAF FORM
Upper: Lanceolate;
Lower: Ovate

POLLINATED BY
Long-tongued insects
like butterflies,
moths and bees

NOTE
Poisonous if ingested;
should not be used on
broken skin

CONSERVATION STATUS
Scarce in its wild form,
possibly due to over-
collection as a medicinal
herb, and is protected in
many parts of Europe

STEMS The stems are stout, round and downy and sparse in leaf.

LEAVES Bright green toothed leaves; upper leaves are opposite, small and lanceolate, lower more clustered and ovate.

FLOWERS Each stem holds one to three orange/yellow daisy-like hermaphrodite flowers surrounded by soft downy sepals.

SEEDS The seeds are 2mm long dark-grey achene with long bristles.

LAUNCH SEEDBOMBS Autumn (a period of cold stratification aids germination).

GERMINATION TIME 2–7 weeks.

HARVESTING SEEDS Fruits ripen late summer/early autumn and look like dandelion clocks.

PLANT CARE Shelter from the wind reduces damage and subsequent disease problems like crown rot. It is unnecessary to feed arnica because its natural environment is usually nutrient deficient. Divide plants in spring and replant immediately.

PESTS AND DISEASES Can be attacked by caterpillars, slugs and snails. Generally disease-free.

CULINARY AND MEDICINAL USES Arnica is not edible and is poisonous if ingested. The roots and the dried flowers are used to make ointments to help treat of bruises and sprains, rheumatism, phlebitis and skin inflammations and to soothe common aches and pains.

Basil

Ocimum basilicum

Basil is a perennial herb native to tropical parts of Asia, grown for its aromatic sweet leaves, which are used in many dishes raw or cooked. It is a member of the *Lamiaceae* family, and it is closely related to many other popular herbs, such as mint and thyme.

FAMILY
Lamiaceae

NATIVE TO
Asia and Africa

HEIGHT/SPREAD
30–60cm x 30–60cm

HABITAT
Containers and raised beds

THRIVES IN
A warm, sheltered sunny position. Highly frost sensitive.

SOIL
Well-drained, fertile soil

LIFESPAN
Annual

FLOWERS
June–August

FORM
Herbaceous

LEAF FORM
Ovate or lanceolate

POLLINATED BY
Self-fertile and small flying insects

NOTE
Overwatering can cause disease

CONSERVATION STATUS
No known conservation issues

STEMS Square stems with leaves that grow on opposite sides.

LEAVES Glossy green, rounded slightly cupped, curving to form a point at the tip.

FLOWERS Small, usually white lipped trumpet-like and arranged along a spike growing from the tip of the stem.

SEEDS Oval black shiny seeds.

LAUNCH SEEDBOMBS From March–June.

GERMINATION TIME 5 days

HARVESTING SEEDS The seeds are contained in the spent flower head. As the seed coat hardens, it changes colour from pale green to brown to black. Cut off the flowerheads and lie on some paper and let them dry for a few days in a warm, dry location. Crush the heads over the colander and separate the chaff.

PLANT CARE Choose a warm, sheltered spot if you are growing it outside, in full sun, in a free-draining soil, pH 5.5–6.5. To promote bushy growth, harvest leaves frequently and pinch off the stem directly above a pair of leaves.

PESTS AND DISEASES Aphids, slugs and snails are all potential pests. Can suffer from Fusarium wilt.

CULINARY AND MEDICINAL USES The sweet, peppery flavour is used in salads, perfect in tomato and cheese-based dishes. It is believed to have strong antioxidant and antimicrobial activity.

Coriander

Coriandrum sativum

This aromatic, annual herb is native to Eurasia and belongs to the *Apiaceae* family, with relatives such as carrot and fennel. Its leaves are used in salads, curries and soups, and the seeds are widely used as a culinary spice, either crushed, ground or whole.

FAMILY
Apiaceae//Umbelliferae

NATIVE TO
Mediterranean and Middle East regions

HEIGHT/SPREAD
20–50 cm x 20–50cm

HABITAT
Containers and raised beds

THRIVES IN
Full sun or partial shade

SOIL
Most well-drained soils

LIFESPAN
Annual

FLOWERS
Spring/Summer

FORM
Bushy

LEAF FORM
Lobed (feathery)

POLLINATED BY
Bees and other pollinators

NOTE
If you see a flower stalk beginning to grow, trim it off to prolong leaf growth. However, if you're hoping to harvest seeds, you'll want to let the flower stalk grow

CONSERVATION STATUS
No known conservation issues

STEMS Green soft aromatic stems used to flavour food.

LEAVES Delicate lace like rounded serrated highly aromatic leaves. They are broadly lobed at the base of the plant, and slender and feathery higher up on the flowering stems..

FLOWERS There are five petals on each white or pale pink flower, forming clusters in an umbrella-like shape called an umbel. The blossoms have a lacy decorative appearance with a faint aroma and a mild flavour similar to the leaves.

SEEDS From March–April

LAUNCH SEEDBOMBS March–June.

GERMINATION TIME 7-10 days

HARVESTING SEEDS Harvest as soon as the seed is brown, dry and aromatic. The seeds fall readily from the seed head so it is a good idea to cover bunches of about 6 heads together in a paper bag and hang them upside-down in warm, dry and airy place. Alternatively, rub the heads together in your hands over a bucket, then place the gathered seed on a tray of newspaper to dry further. Winnow the chaff and store in an airtight container.

PLANT CARE Grow in a light and fertile, well-drained soil, pH 6.5–7.5. For seed production, the plants are best in full sun; for better leaves, grow in partial shade. Keep watering to a minimum. The leaves can be picked at any time.

PESTS AND DISEASES Aphids and rust.

CULINARY AND MEDICINAL USES Coriander makes a useful addition to the kitchen garden. It bears flavoursome, feathery leaves and flat flower heads. Coriander is said to reduce flatulence and increase appetite, and a poultice made from the plant is believed to relieve rheumatism and painful joints.

Papalo

Porophyllum ruderale

A fast-growing, hardy, annual herb from South America. It reaches 60cm tall. The name comes from papalotl, the local word for butterfly, because the flowers attract butterflies. Papalo is an unusual herb in the *Asteraceae* family, whose members include lettuce and dandelion.

STEMS Tall, branching slender upright fibrous green stems.

LEAVES Ranging from blue-green to dark green, they are sturdy, broad, smooth and flat with scalloped edges.

FLOWERS Purplish brownish green bursts of dandelion-like flowers.

SEEDS Similar shape to dandelion seeds, having a brown stalk and feathery umbrella to help them travel by wind.

LAUNCH SEEDBOMBS Spring.

GERMINATION TIME 7–14 days

HARVESTING SEEDS Autumn.

PLANT CARE They grow quite well in the wild, making them really easy to grow in your garden.

PESTS AND DISEASES Thought to be a pest repellent. Generally disease-free.

CULINARY AND MEDICINAL USES The leaves have a distinctive, spicy-sharp aroma and are eaten raw in sandwiches, salsas and salads. Add at the last minute to cooked dishes like soups and stews. It is best used fresh. Papalo is believed to be helpful in treating liver ailments as well as high blood pressure.

Hollyhock

Alcea rosea

Native to western Asia, hollyhock, like okra, belongs to the *Malvaceae* family. The plant is, at best, a short-lived perennial, sometimes behaving like an annual or biennial. When in flower, hollyhocks can reach up to 2.5m tall, depending on variety.

FAMILY
Malvaceae

NATIVE TO
China

HEIGHT/SPREAD
2/1m

HABITAT
Coastal, domestic gardens, urban weed.

THRIVES IN
Full sun

SOIL
Most well drained soils

LIFESPAN
Biennial or short-lived perennial

FLOWERS
June–August

FORM
Columnar upright

LEAF FORM
Shallowly lobed, rounded

POLLINATED BY
Bees, hummingbirds and butterflies

NOTE
Seek the advice from a qualified herbalist before using

CONSERVATION STATUS
No known conservation issues

STEMS Tough woody stem with thick silver hairs..

LEAVES Alternate, heart-shaped soft fuzzy leaves that clump up into a mound below the flower stalks.

FLOWERS Long erect racemes of open funnel-shaped pink, purple, red, white or yellow flowers up to 10 cm in diameter.

SEEDS Disk-like thin brown seeds form stacked in a circular donut-shaped pod.

LAUNCH SEEDBOMBS Spring.

GERMINATION TIME 7–30 days

HARVESTING SEEDS When the spent flower petals fall a plump green donut-like shaped pod forms at the bottom of the flower. When it turns yellowish-brown the top will open and the seeds will become visible. Gently pick the seeds apart from each other and dry out on paper for a couple of days.

PLANT CARE Grow in full sun in well-drained soil, pH 6.0–8.0. The plants are reliably drought resistant.

PESTS AND DISEASES At risk from aphids, capsid bugs, cutworm, flea beetle, slugs, snails and rust.

CULINARY AND MEDICINAL USES
Hollyhock is completely edible – leaves, roots, flowers and seeds. The young soft leaves can be used as spinach. The flowers can be added to salads. It can also be used in skin care. Steep flowers in warm water, crush a little and apply directly to dry areas on your face. The flowers can also be added to a bath to help to soothe any dry skin.

Honesty

Lunaria annua

A biennial plant native to Eurasia, honesty is from the *Brassicaceae* family, whose members include cabbage and turnip. The papery, pearly, moon-like seed pods, which appear in summer not long after the flowers have faded, inspire its Latin genus name, *Lunaria*.

FAMILY
Brassicaceae

NATIVE TO
Central and Southern Europe

HEIGHT/SPREAD
100 x 30cm

HABITAT
Flower beds. This garden escapee can often be found on waste ground, railway cuttings and roadside verges and naturalised along paths, woodlands, field edges and hedgerows.

THRIVES IN
Full sun to partial shade

SOIL
Fertile, moist and well-drained, slightly alkaline soil

LIFESPAN
Biennial

FLOWERS
April–May

FORM
Branched

LEAF FORM
Ovate with a pointed end

POLLINATED BY
Butterflies, moths, and bees and flies are self-fertile

NOTE
Can become invasive if left to its own devices

CONSERVATION STATUS
Introduced, non-native

STEMS Square hairy branched stems.
LEAVES Rich green heart-shaped leaves with toothed edges.
FLOWERS Hermaphrodite (has both male and female organs) clusters of cruciforme (cross shaped) fragrant white or purple flowers growing all over the tall, branched stems.
SEEDS Flat coin shaped, translucent papery pods, hold the dark disk-like seeds. The pods are often used in dried flower arranging but I prefer to see them adding winter interest to the garden.
LAUNCH SEEDBOMBS Early summer to flower the following spring.

GERMINATION TIME 7–14 days
HARVESTING SEEDS August–October.
PLANT CARE Grow in full sun or partial shade, in a well-drained, yet moisture-retentive soil, pH 5.6–7.5. Overwinter in the garden for seed collection.
PESTS AND DISEASES No pests but at risk from clubroot.
CULINARY AND MEDICINAL USES
In the same family as cabbage and mustard it shares the same pungent flavour.
The seeds can be toasted and used as a mustard substitute. Use the root to make a horseradish sauce and the flowers and leaves in salads. No known medical uses.

Love-in-a-mist

Nigella sativa

This pretty annual flower, native to Eurasia and belonging to the *Ranunculaceae* family, is valued for its seeds.

FAMILY
Ranunculaceae

NATIVE TO
Northern Africa, southern Europe and southwest Asia

HEIGHT/SPREAD
60 x 60cm

HABITAT
Domestic gardens, fields, roadsides and in rocky or waste ground

THRIVES IN
Full sun/partial shade

SOIL
Any well-drained soil

LIFESPAN
Annual

FLOWERS
Late Spring–Autumn

FORM
Upright and bushy

LEAF FORM
Pinnately divided

POLLINATED BY
Bees and insects

NOTE
Can be invasive in some areas

CONSERVATION STATUS
No known conservation issues

STEMS Light green, erect and sparsely branched with alternate leaves and often with a terminal flower growing at the tip.

LEAVES Light green feathery, lace-like, alternate leaves that give the impression of "mist" surrounding the jewel-like flowers.

FLOWERS Bright blue, pale blue, white, pink, or lavender flowers that have 5 large petal-like sepals and small, deeply divided petals hidden beneath the stamens.

SEEDS The plant self-seeds and continues to grow in the same spot year after year. The seeds are jet black and textured with tiny dots forming stripes or veins.

LAUNCH SEEDBOMBS Autumn and suitable for winter sowing.

GERMINATION TIME 7–14 days

HARVESTING SEEDS The seeds form in a bulbous pod with purple stripes. Openings appear as the pod dries and fall out as the wind blows. Harvest when the stripes are still visible and hang pods upside down in a paper bag for the seed to fall into. The decorative seed pods can be used in fresh or dried floral arrangements.

PLANT CARE Grow in full sun or partial shade in free-draining soil, pH 6.6–7.5.

PESTS AND DISEASES Generally pest- and disease-free.

CULINARY AND MEDICINAL USES
The seeds, often called 'Black Cumin' can be eaten raw or cooked. They are thought to be antidiabetic, antimicrobial and anti-inflammatory.

"LOOK DEEP INTO NATURE,
AND THEN YOU WILL UNDERSTAND
EVERYTHING BETTER."

Albert Einstein

Primrose

Primula vulgaris

These hardy perennials from the *Primulaceae* family are native to Eurasia. They are a highly valued spring flower, with pretty pale yellow flowers, although many cultivated forms are available in whites, pinks, purples, yellows and bi-colours.

FAMILY
Primulaceae

NATIVE TO
Western Europe to North Africa and West Asia

HEIGHT/SPREAD
30 x 30cm

HABITAT
Woods, ancient woodland, hedgerows and bogs

THRIVES IN
Full sun/partial shade/ full shade

SOIL
Moist soil/can tolerate boggy clay and maritime

LIFESPAN
Perennial

FLOWERS
December–May

FORM
Ground Cover

LEAF FORM
Pinnate leaves

POLLINATED BY
Bees, moths & butterflies

NOTE
Not to be used if pregnant

CONSERVATION STATUS
Protected in Northern Ireland under the Wildlife Order, 1985

STEMS Wooly short upright single stem.

LEAVES Heavily wrinkled, unevenly toothed tongue-like leaves grow from a basal rosette.

FLOWERS The pale yellow with darker yellow-orange centres delicately scented Hermaphrodite (has both male and female organs) have five notched petals and are among the first to appear in spring, born singly on the ends of upright woolly stems.

SEEDS The seeds are tiny brown balls. Several seeds are contained in the seedpod.

LAUNCH SEEDBOMBS July–August.

GERMINATION TIME 3–24 weeks

HARVESTING SEEDS April–August. The unripe seed pod is a shiny ball containing soft white seeds, when ripe the seeds turn hard and brown or black. Sow immediately so that winter dormancy doesn't set in.

PLANT CARE Grow in full sun or partial shade, in moist but well-drained soil, pH 5.5–7.0, enriched with plenty of leaf mould. Mulch during the summer to keep the roots cool. These are great little plants to grow in damp areas as they love moist soil.

PESTS AND DISEASES Aphids, slugs, snails, crown rot and grey mould.

CULINARY AND MEDICINAL USES With its slightly bitter lettuce flavour, young leaves and flowers, cooked or raw, can be added to salads and soups or made into a syrup and used as a tea. The flowers can also make wine. Traditionally used to help treat conditions involving spasms, cramps and rheumatic pains.

Sunflower

Helianthus annuus

Native to the Americas, sunflowers were originally cultivated by North American Indians for their nutritious seeds. A member of the *Asteraceae* family along with all other daisy flowers, this annual plant is well loved for its sunshine-like flowers.

STEMS Rough, hairy woody.

LEAVES Broad, coarsely toothed, rough and growing alternately up the stem, getting smaller the higher up they grow. The leaves at the base of the plant are arranged opposite. The leaves have serrated edges, are 10–30cm long and range from triangular to heart-shaped, they have hairs on the upper and underside.

FLOWERS The flower heads consist of numerous small individual five-petaled florets. The outer flowers resemble petals and are called ray flowers. Sunflowers are Hermaphrodite. The flowers in the centre of the head are called disk flowers and are arranged in a spiral, they mature into seeds.

SEEDS Ripen from September–October.

LAUNCH SEEDBOMBS Early spring in pots and mid spring in situ.

GERMINATION TIME 14 days

HARVESTING SEEDS The seeds are ripe when the flower heads start to dry and turn to face the ground. Cut off flower heads keeping 20cm of the stem attached and hang them upside down inside a pillow case. After a few days you can rub the seeds out gently with your hand or a brush or if you have two seed heads try rubbing them together.

PLANT CARE Grow in full sun, in fertile, moist but well-drained soil, pH 5.7–8.5. Sunflowers are happy in dry, poor to average soil and need little water or fertilizer.

PESTS AND DISEASES Banded sunflower moth, cutworm, slugs, snails, downy mildew, powdery mildew, rust.

CULINARY AND MEDICINAL USES The seeds have a delicious nut-like flavour and are rich in fats so can be made into oil or butter or ground up and used in baking. The sprouted seeds can be eaten raw. A tea made from the leaves is thought to be useful as an astringent, diuretic or expectorant.

FAMILY
Asteraceae

NATIVE TO
North and South America

HEIGHT/SPREAD
3m/30cm

HABITAT
Open dry Agricultural fields and domestic gardens

THRIVES IN
Full sun

SOIL
Most soils but prefers well-drained soil and can tolerate drought

LIFESPAN
Annual

FLOWERS
July–September

FORM
Upright single flower or branched with many flowers (wild)

LEAF FORM
Petiolate, dentate

POLLINATED BY
Bees and flies

NOTE
When grown as a crop plant it can accumulate nitrates from artificial fertilisers which when consumed, may cause allergic reactions

CONSERVATION STATUS
No known conservation issues

Wild Yarrow

Achillea millefolium

A perennial wildflower native to Eurasia, Wild Yarrow belongs to the *Asteraceae* family. It has pleasantly aromatic, feathery foliage that has long been used as a herbal medicine to treat wounds, colds and digestive complaints. In the wild, it thrives in fields and along fence lines and roadsides.

FAMILY
Asteraceae

NATIVE TO
Eurasia

HEIGHT/SPREAD
50 x 50cm

HABITAT
Meadows, ground cover, lawns, roadside verges, downland

THRIVES IN
Full sun/partial shade

SOIL
Well drained, sandy, loamy, clay

LIFESPAN
Herbaceous perennial

FLOWERS
June–November

FORM
Bushy

LEAF FORM
Bipinnate/tripinnate

POLLINATED BY
Insects

NOTE
Extended use of Yarrow can cause allergic skin rashes or lead to photosensitivity in some people.

CONSERVATION STATUS
No known conservation issues

STEMS Grooved with small wooly hairs.
LEAVES The dark green, finely divided, feathery lace-like alternate leaves are 5–20cm long and are covered in fine hairs..
FLOWERS Strong-smelling clusters of white, flat-topped flower heads each composed of many small flowers.
SEEDS Tiny silver, long, slightly pear-shaped seeds.
LAUNCH SEEDBOMBS Early spring or autumn.
GERMINATION TIME 7–30 days
HARVESTING SEEDS Seed is ready to harvest when the flowers have dried brown, place them in a paper bag and leave to dry for a week then gently rub or brush the seeds out onto a piece of newspaper.

PLANT CARE Grow in full sun or partial shade. Yarrow is drought tolerant and prefers poor, well-drained soil, pH 4.7–8.0.
PESTS AND DISEASES Aphids and powdery mildew.
CULINARY AND MEDICINAL USES
Used as a hop substitute for flavouring beer. The flowers and leaves can be steeped to make an aromatic tea and the young leaves can be added to salads, though they have a bitter flavour. Traditionally used to help treat wounds and stop blood flow, it is believed to help alleviate kidney problems, colds, fevers and menstrual pain and many other disorders. Can also be used as a pest deterrent and burned to ward off mosquitos.

Q&A

Q What do I do if my seeds go mouldy?

A It is likely that they have been exposed to moisture and may no longer be fit for storage. I'd suggest sowing them and seeing what happens! Always make sure there is good aeration when drying seeds, and that when the seeds are fully dry, they are stored in an airtight container.

Q How do I know if my seeds are still alive?

A You can test the seeds by placing them in water. Generally, viable seeds will sink and non-viable seeds will float. Alternatively, you could test them by sowing and seeing what happens.

Q What do I do if my seedlings develop rot?

A This is due to overwatering. Unfortunately, there is no chance of saving the seedlings, so the best thing to do is to compost the plants and start again with fresh seeds.

Q How do I know when a seed head is fully mature?

A All plants mature in different ways, but the tell-tale signs are the same: the seed head will turn brown, dry out and eventually release its seeds. It's helpful if you're able to observe the maturity process for one year and make notes; you'll be better informed the following year and so able to capture the seeds when they are ready and before they release into the garden.

Q Do I need lots of space to dry seeds?

A Swap your surplus seeds once you have saved and stored enough for your own future use. Never swap seeds that you haven't already saved a batch of; there's nothing worse than wishing you hadn't given seeds away when you later find a use for them.

Q What should I do if it all goes wrong?

A The fear of it all going wrong – of, essentially, killing plants – is, I think, something that puts people off gardening.

My advice to bear in mind is that you are working with the plants' desire to live: if it has a strong desire, it will withstand the harshest of conditions. Your role is to do what you can to provide good growing conditions, but don't beat yourself up if there are a few fatalities along the way. Learn from your mistakes, jot them down, and do something different the next time. Remember to enjoy working with plants and that nature will always guide you.

Making Seedbombs

Q What do I do if the mixture I make is too sticky to roll into a ball?

A Either add more earth or leave the mixture to dry for a while.

Q Should larger seeds be treated differently when making seedbombs?

A If you are using larger seeds, such as beans, make the earth casing bigger and use fewer seeds.

Q What do I do if I accidentally forget to put the seeds in before the water?

A The seeds are usually added to the dry 'mix' because they blend with the earth more evenly. Don't worry, however – just add the seeds and stir in gently but thoroughly.

Q What happens if the seedbombs go a bit mouldy when they are drying?

A It could be because your 'drying place' is too humid. Wipe off the mould with a damp cloth and relocate to a drier place, such as above a radiator.

Q Do the seedbombs have to be dry before you launch them?

A No. If the time of year is right for the seed to be sown, you can launch them immediately. The moisture content will make germination more rapid.

Q How do I store the seedbombs?

A They can be stored when they are completely dry in an airtight container or even paper bags in a dry place for later use.

Launching Seedbombs

Q How do I know when to launch them?

A Read the information provided with your seeds.

Q Why isn't my seedbomb germinating?

A Maybe it is too dry. A good water will dissolve it a bit and let the light in.

Q Will all the seeds germinate?

A It's likely some will germinate this season and some the following seasons.

Q Do the seedbombs need aftercare once launched?

A If you can reach them or are growing them as a crop it would be prudent to keep them watered and even give them a liquid feed once in a while. Do some thinning-out if necessary.

Picture Credits

Glossary

ABSCISIC ACID A plant hormone that plays an important role in plant development, including dormancy.

ACHENE A dry one-seeded fruit, which does not open to release the seed.

ADVENTITIOUS ROOT Root that arises from the stem and not from another root.

ALTERNATE Each leaf grows alternately one at a time along the stem.

ANNUAL Life cycle lasts one season.

ARABLE Land capable of being cultivated.

AXIL Where the leaf joins the stem.

BIENNIAL Completes life cycle in two seasons, germinating and growing the first season and flowering and setting seed in the second.

BIODIVERSITY The variety of life in the world.

BIOTECHNOLOGY Manufacturing or technological engineering that uses living organisms.

BIPINNATIFID Pinnate leaves with doubly cut segments.

BOLTING Usually referring to

vegetables when they send up a flower stalk too quickly. This means the plant has gone to seed early and often results in a much lower yield and an inferior flavour.

BRACT A modified leaf protecting the flower.

BROADCAST SEEDS The method of casting seeds over a broad area, onto pre-prepared ground.

BULB An underground modified bud and stem used as a food storage organ by dormant plants.

CALCAREOUS Lime-rich.

CHLOROPHYLL Green photosynthetic pigment responsible for trapping radiant light.

CHLOROPLAST The portion of a plant cell that contains chlorophyll.

CLOCHE A protective cover for outdoor plants.

COLD FRAME An unheated frame with a glass or plastic top where small plants and seedlings are hardened off.

COMPOUND A flower made up of numerous florets.

CROSS BREEDING The mating of two distinctly different varieties or species of plants to produce

a hybrid, or cross breed. Cross breeding can occur naturally, or artifi cially by human intervention.

CROSS-POLLINATE The transfer of pollen between two different plants.

CRYOPRESERVATION The preservation of living organisms by cooling them to extremely low temperatures.

CUT-AND-COME-AGAIN Describes edible leafy plants where the leaves are cut while the plant is still growing in the ground. The leaves then re-grow (come again).

CYME Flat-topped cluster of flowers.

DAMPING OFF A lifethreatening disease of seedlings caused by a variety of fungi.

DEADHEADING The removal of dead or spent fl owers from a plant. Deadheading prevents the formation of seed heads.

DIFFUSION The movement of fluid from an area of higher concentration to an area of lower concentration until a balance is reached.

DIOECIOUS Male and female reproductive organs found on

separate plants.

DISC FLORET Small tubular petal-like flower at the centre of the flower head.

ECOSYSTEM The complete biological activity and interaction of a community of organisms within an area.

ENVIRONMENTALIST Someone who works toward protecting and improving the natural environment

ENZYMES Complex chemicals produced by plant cells, which help activate processes such as photosynthesis.

EPIPHYTIC A plant that grows on another for support.

ETHNOBOTANY The study of plants and their relationships with human society.

EVERGREEN A plant that retains its leaves all year round.

FILIAL GENERATION A generation of offspring produced from cross breeding genetically different plants. The fi rst generation is referred to as the F1 generation, followed by the F2 generation, and so on.

FLORET Tiny flower.

GENETIC DRIFT The change in the genetic variety of a population over time due to the random passing on of genes from one population to the next. This usually only affects smaller populations, as the diversity weakens over time.

GERMINATION Transition of seed to seedling.

GLABROUS Smooth, lacking hairs or bristles.

HABIT The general appearance of a plant; for example, spreading, upright, bushy or creeping.

HERBACEOUS Non-woody plants whose leaves and stems die down at the end of the growing season.

HERBARIUM A collection of preserved plant specimens.

HERBICIDE A chemical or organic-based agent used to kill unwanted plants.

HERMAPHRODITE Male and female organs found on the same flower.

HETEROPHYLLY Plants that have leaves of different shapes on the same plant.

INDIGENOUS Native to a particular region.

INSECTICIDE Chemical or organic-based agent used to control damaging insects.

INTERBREEDING When two genetically similar plants mate.

IN-VITRO An experimental process performed outside a living organism in an artifi cial environment such as a test tube.

INVOLUCRE A protective whorl of bracts surrounding a flower.

LEPIDOPTERA Moths and butterflies.

LIQUID NITROGEN Nitrogen in liquid form, used for freezing.

LOBED Deeply indented leaves.

MERICARP A single, separating part of a manyseeded dry fruit.

MIDRIB A strong central leaf vein.

MONOECIOUS Male and female reproductive organs found on the same plant.

NODE A point on the stem where the leaves emerge.

NODULE An outgrowth from the roots of legumes containing nitrogen-fixing bacteria.

OBLANCEOLATE Lanceshaped but with the widest part at the tip of the leaf and the narrowest at the base.

OBLONG A leaf with a length greater than the width.

ORBICULAR Circular.

OBLONGOID An elongated circle.

ORGANISM An independent living thing.

PANICLE Branched compound flower of racemes arranged around the main floral stem.

PAPPUS A covering of scales; feathery hairs or bristles at the apex of the seed.

PARASITIC WASP Wasp that feeds on pest insects.

PATENT LAWS A written law concerned with ownership rights.

PERENNIAL A plant that lasts for more than two growing seasons.

PESTICIDE A chemical substance used to kill pests, especially insects.

PH A measure of the acidity or alkalinity of a soil or solution, on a scale of 0 to 14, where 7 is neutral. A value above 7 is alkaline, and a value below 7 is acidic.

PINNATE A leaf made of leaflets arranged in a row on either side of the midrib.

PINNATIPARTITE A leaf with incisioned lobes extending over halfway toward the midrib.

RACEME A cluster of tightly packed flowers growing in long thin columns (e.g. foxglove); the flowers at the base open first.

RAY FLORET The petal-like outer floret of a flower head (e.g. sunflower).

RECEPTACLE Swollen area at the stem tip where the flower grows.

REFLEXED Bent downwards and turned backwards.

REPOPULATE To introduce a number of species into an area especially with the aim to rebuild or sustain a population.

RHIZOME An underground horizontal stem that sends out roots and shoots.

ROOT BALL The clump of roots of a container-grown plant, consisting of the roots and soil.

ROSETTE A low-growing circular arrangement of leaves.

RUNNER Horizontal stem sent out from the base of a plant, which produces new plants from buds along the stem and at the tips.

SCARIFICATION Cutting the seed coat to encourage germination by allowing water to penetrate the seed.

SEED DRILL A shallow trench into which seeds are sown.

SEED SOVEREIGNTY Power over seed supply. This has moved progressively from farmers to seed companies since the 1930s.

SELF-FERTILE Capable of self-fertilization without the need for another plant.

SELF-POLLINATE The fertilization of a flower by its own pollen, from its anthers to its stigma.

SELF-SEED A plant naturally regenerated from seed without human intervention.

SEPALS Modified leaves that occur outside the petals and protect the flower bud.

SILIQUA A long dry seed capsule with a central partition to which the seeds are attached.

STRATIFICATION Pretreating seeds to help germination by simulating natural winter conditions, e.g. freezing.

SOIL TYPE Classification of soil based on its sand, silt, clay and organic matter content and pH.

SPATULATE Broad and rounded at the top with a narrow base.

SPURRED A spiked part of a flower.

SUBSHRUB A low-growing woody perennial.

SUBSOIL The soil between topsoil and bedrock.

TERMINATOR TECHNOLOGY The use of genetic technology to create plants that produce sterile seeds, which are incapable of producing further offspring.

TRANSITION TOWN INITIATIVE A community-led process that helps a village, town or city become stronger through initiatives to improve areas such as food transport and energy.

TRIFOLIATE A leaf divided into three leaflets.

TRIPINNATE A leaf divided three times, as in ferns.

TRUE SEEDS Those that retain the distinguishing characteristics of their parents.

UMBEL A multiplestemmed umbrellashaped cluster of flowers.

UMBELLIFEROUS Plants belonging to the *Umbelliferae* family, or plants that produce umbels, i.e. flat-topped flower heads composed of many short stalks originating from the tip of a central stem.

WHORL Arrangement of leaves, petals, etc. in a circular or spiral pattern.

VEGETATIVE PROPAGATION Asexual reproduction of plants through cuttings, division, runners.

VIABLE (of seeds) Able to germinate.

Index

Acknowledgements

I dedicate this book to my family, for giving me the support to flourish as a person, and to my three beautiful sons who now have a love for gardening.

To Steve, for always believing that I can do it and for listening to me sound out my ideas and geeky passions without making me feel silly! To my lovely Mum, who is always such a source of inspiration and my Dad, who is always such a source of amusement! To my siblings, Amy and Azza and Rose for their support and love! To my in-laws Brian and Sheila, for their strength and for being wonderful parents and grandparents. To my friends, as always, I thank them for their support and belief in me, those in Wales, Brighton and beyond!

And forever more I will dedicate all the good that I do to my sister Holly, the most beautiful flower in heaven's garden xxxx

I would also like to thank: Monica Perdoni, for her unshakeable belief in me; Quarto for loving my work; all at Seedy Sunday Brighton; Vandana Shiva for her inspirational work with seeds.

And to all the readers of this book: you are the key to the growing community.

Brimming with creative inspiration, how-to projects, and useful information to enrich your everyday life, quarto.com is a favourite destination for those pursuing their interests and passions.

Some pages first published as *Seedbombs* in 2012 and other text taken from *Seedswap* 2011.

This edition published in 2022 by Leaping Hare Press
An imprint of the Quarto Publishing Group
The Old Brewery, 6 Blundell street
London N7 9BH, United Kingdom
T (0)20 7700 6700
www.Quarto.com

Copyright © 2011, 2012, 2022 Quarto Publishing plc

British Library Cataloguing-in-Publication Data A catalogue record for this book is available from the British Library

ISBN 978-0-7112-7539-3
E-book ISBN 978-0-7112-7540-9

10 9 8 7 6 5 4 3 2 1

Publisher: Monica Perdoni
Art Director: Isabel Eeles
Designer: Sally Bond
Editor and Picture Research: Nayima Ali
Production: Maeve Healy
Cover Design: Tina Smith Hobson

Printed in China